THE *Amazing* JOHNNY RABBITT *St. Louis* TRIVIA GAME

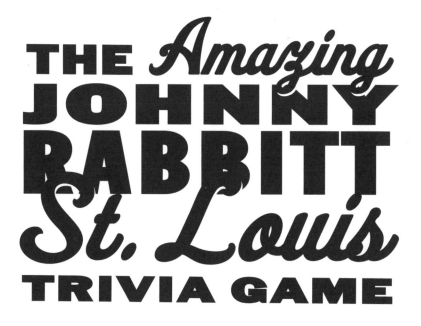

THE AMAZING *Johnny Rabbitt*
ST. LOUIS TRIVIA GAME

Printed in the United States of America.

First Edition.

ISBN 1-891442-43-0

Library of Congress number 2006931830

Virginia Publishing Company
P.O. Box 4538
St. Louis MO 63108
(314) 367-6612
www.stl-books.com
Please check out our Web site for other books on St. Louis history.

Book cover and interior design by Michael Kilfoy
with assistance by Ryan Asher
of Studio X, St. Louis, MO
(314) 773-8900 www.studiox.us

Johnny Rabbitt cover caricature by R. J. Shay

Back cover photograph taken by Suzy Gorman

Edited by Fran Levy

CREDIT WHERE CREDIT IS DUE

This second Johnny Rabbitt St. Louis Trivia Book, as was the first, has been a true labor of love for our town. I sincerely hope you enjoy it and that it'll help you win some rounds at trivia nights.

In the creation of this work, well over 150 books, documents and periodicals were consulted as references; and there was the invaluable assistance of many, including St. Louis scholars Andy "Prof. Tigger" Rochman, Ben Hilliker, Steve De Bellis, Lemay Fire Chief Neil Svetanics and the late Norbury Wayman. I appreciate all the efforts of Michael Kilfoy and RJ Shay of Studio X and the guidance and input of Jeff Fister and Kimberly Clark Marlowe of Virginia Publishing. And special thanks to my wife, Gwen, for putting up with my ongoing investigations, stacks of papers and countless notes scattered through the house. She urged me on each day by saying: "Are you working on that damn book, again?!"

Oh, by the way, the Internet was not used for any of the research on this book.

Yours truly,

Johnny Rabbitt, AKA RON ELZ

I'd read all the questions and answers as this work progressed to the best listener ever, to whom this book is dedicated. My very special friend *"Mazie The Dog,"* our 5-year-old Irish Wheaten Terrier.

Johnny Rabbitt, AKA RON ELZ

Table of Contents

★ JOHNNY RABBITT TRIVIA GAME ★

Round One: PEOPLE, PLACES AND STUFF 9

Round Two: A COLLECTION OF QUESTIONS 12

Round Three: IN OUR TOWN 15

Memories: 1947: THE BEGINNING OF PROMTIME 21

Round Four: BE A GOOD SPORT 26

Round Five: EAT, DRINK & BE HAPPY 30

Round Six: GONE, BUT (HOPEFULLY) NOT FORGOTTEN 37

Memories: AIRWAVES 41

Round Seven: SOMEWHERE THERE'S MUSIC 45

Round Eight: ON THE AIR 50

Round Nine: PARKS 59

Memories: 1969 61

Round Ten: THE SWINGIN' SIXTIES 65

Round Eleven: WHO, WHAT, WHERE, WHEN? 69

Memories: THE BEATLES STORY, CHAPTER ONE 72

Round Twelve: RIDE ON! 73

Round Thirteen: SEE WHAT YOU KNOW! 76

Memories: THE BEATLES STORY, CHAPTER TWO 80

Round Fourteen: SHAW'S GARDEN 81

Round Fifteen: SHOPPING IN THE TWILIGHT ZONE 84
Memories: THE BEATLES STORY, CHAPTER THREE 88
Round Sixteen: TRIVIAMANIA 89
Round Seventeen: PAST TIMES 95
Round Eighteen: 1904 - THE FAIR YEAR 99
*Memories:*THE BEATLES STORY, CHAPTER FOUR 103
Round Nineteen: THE SEARCH IS ON! 105
Round Twenty: THE SHOW MUST GO ON 109
Round Twenty-One: THE 20'S ROAR 112
Memories: THE BEATLES STORY, CHAPTER FIVE 114
Round Twenty-Two: ST. LOUIS TRIVIA 101 115
Round Twenty-Three: WE MEAN BUSINESS! 119
Round Twenty-Four: TRIVIARAMA 122
Round Twenty-Five: LOOKIN' BACK, WAY BACK 128
Memories: THE ST. LOUIS PICTURE SHOW 131
About the Author: ST. LOUIS' OWN JOHNNY RABBITT 136

Editor's Note

If you would like to play along, just cover the page with a sheet of paper, then slide it down to read the question and then, unveil the answer. It's easy and fun.

RABBITT'S TRIVIA GAME

People, Places and Stuff

★ ROUND ONE ★

1. The City of Berkeley municipal swimming pool (circa 1955) is in what subdivision?

Frostwood

2. The Central West End annual house and garden tours began during what decade of the 20th century?

The 1960s (1969)

3. Which "dime store" was one of the original anchors for the Hampton Village Shopping Center at Hampton Ave. and Chippewa St.?

S. S. Kresge

4. Name the St. Louis TV sports director who has held that title for the longest period of time?

Rich Gould (KPLR)

5. Before the Famous-Barr name was retired by Macy's, what was the final F-B slogan?

Always Something Exciting

6. "Makes Everything Taste Better" is a phrase found on what area landmark sign?

The Brooks Catsup water tower in Collinsville

7. "The Alexa" condos is the new name for the Chemical Building downtown. In addition to a new name, the building got a new address: 777 Olive St. What was the structure's original address?

721 Olive St.

8. What radio station was for a time located in the REJIS (Regional Justice Information Service) building at 4255 W. Pine Blvd.?

KXOK

9. What was the name of the cocktail lounge and show room at the original Alton Belle Casino (now Argosy Casino)?

Ace's

10. In the 1976 John Lutz St. Louis-based novel *Buyer Beware,* what was the name of the place in which his character, private investigator Alo Nudger, lived?

Trailer Haven

11. Where in St. Louis will you find a replica of the tomb of King Mausolus, one of the Seven Wonders of the ancient world?

Atop the Civil Courts building at 1200 Market Street

12. Jules Jablonow headed what yesteryear St. Louis-based movie theatre chain?

Mid-America Theatres

13. The Mosaics Museum is located in what building?

The Cathedral Basilica of St. Louis

14. What institution created the Water Tower Inn hotel?

St. Louis University

15. The current Pageant Theatre is located in the 6100 block of Delmar Blvd. In what block of Delmar was the first Pageant Theatre?

5800 (5851)

16. What was the original name of the music club that became Mississippi Nights?

On The Rocks

17. The nightclub "Finale" at Bonhomme Ave. and Brentwood Blvd. in Clayton was the concept of what individual?

Steve Schankman, head of Contemporary Productions

18. What brand of coffee is used in Schlafly Brewery's Coffee Stout?

Kaldi's

19. Who was the first St. Louis magician to be named National President of The Society of American Magicians. This group was founded in 1902.

Harry Monti. (He presided in 1999-2000.)

20. Name the Catholic elementary school (founded in 2003) that is located at the intersection of Arsenal St. and Oregon Ave.

St. Frances Cabrini

21. Who was the owner of the famous Club Imperial ballroom on W. Florissant Ave.?

George Edick

22. What's the name of the small park directly across Grand Blvd. from the Fox Theatre?

Leon Strauss Park

23. Actor Kevin Kline's father, Robert Kline, operated a long-time retail toy and record business from three different locations in Clayton. What was the name of the store?

The Record Bar

24. Suntan Beach was located off what state highway?

Highway 94 in St. Charles County, north of St. Charles City

25. The Broadview Hotel was located in what area city?

E. St. Louis

26. Name the gift shop in the Central West End that closed at the end of April '06 after 27 years in business.

Heffalump's

27. In addition to the *fleur de lis,* what other design is depicted on the reins of the horse held by the figure of King Louis IX in front of the City Art Museum?

Formée cross

RABBITT'S TRIVIA GAME

A Collection of Questions

★ ROUND TWO ★

1. Name the multi-billion dollar company with headquarters adjacent to North Park on the UMSL campus.

   Express Scripts

2. Name the company whose slogan is "The Future Belongs to You."

   American Equity Mortgage

3. Ted Drewes starting selling frozen custard in what year?

   1929 in Florida, 1930 in St. Louis

4. Name the person who was the spiritual leader of the St. Louis Archdiocese from 1903 until his death on March 9, 1946.

   Cardinal John Joseph Glennon (named Cardinal 12/24/45)

5. The late Irma Schira Tucker founded what theatre group as a spin-off of the YMCA's George Williams players?

   The City Players

6. When Southwestern Bell used names for telephone exchanges, what was the name assigned to the designation LO?

   Lockhart

7. The New Town at St. Charles was developed by what residential construction company?

   Whittaker Homes

8. What area community has hosted a Memorial (Decoration) Day parade since 1868, billed as the longest-running such event in the United States?

   Alton

9. What was the original name of the theatre building on Grandel Square that is now known as "The Sun"?

The Victoria, a German-language theatre and meeting facility. It was also known as the Liberty, Liberty Burlesque, Fox Liberty, Club 400 and Lyn. It once housed a fundamentalist revival church, and a short-lived television production workshop, and briefly was home to the Theatre Project Company.

10. Name the Missouri River island once suggested as a site for an airport. It's northwest of the Spirit of St. Louis Airport in Chesterfield.

Howell Island

11. Two men who would become President of the United States each served at Jefferson Barracks. Name them.

Ulysses S. Grant (18th president) and Dwight D. Eisenhower (34th president)

12. When Northwest Plaza opened in 1965, they had four "anchor" stores: Famous-Barr, J. C. Penny, Sears and...what was the fourth?

Scruggs-Vandervoort-Barney

13. Name the St. Louis paint company that had its headquarters at 1823 Washington Ave., a plant in E. St. Louis, and retail stores at 11 locations. Their slogan was "Pre-tested Guaranteed."

Morris Paint & Varnish Co.

14. Who was the St. Louis University basketball coach when the Billikens won the Missouri Valley Conference championship for the first time? (1946-47)?

John P. Flanigan

15. At what university is the Katherine Dunham Center for the Arts and Humanities located?

Southern Illinois University – Edwardsville

16. During the 1950s and early '60s, in what dining and drinking establishment in Midtown would you have found the Lillian Russell Hideaway Bar, the Plume cocktail lounge and the Gilded Cage bar.

Sal Lo Piccolo's Victorian Club at 3719 Washington Ave.

17. There were two Putt-Putt miniature golf courses in St. Louis. One was at 8044 Manchester Rd., just west of Hanley Rd. The other was across from a North County shopping center. What's the name of the center?

Village Square

18. In what institution is Phil the Gorilla's skeleton stored?

It's in a crate at the St. Louis Science Center's storage facility. Phil's stuffed exterior is on display at the Saint Louis Zoo.

19. It's the oldest library west of the Mississippi River and it's located in the St. Louis area. Which library is it?

St. Louis Mercantile Library Association. It's adjacent to the Thomas Jefferson Library on the campus of UMSL.

20. What St. Louis-based airline, which was owned by former dry-cleaner George Calashu, operated with a small fleet of Lear jets?

Sun Airlines

21. For whom is the St. Louis University High School theatre named?

Joseph Schulte, long-time SLUH theatre teacher

22. Which downtown apartment building features steam-spewing lion heads along its cornice?

Bee Hat Apartments – 1021 Washington Avenue

23. In what Sherlock Holmes story will you find a character named Jefferson Hope who was from St. Louis?

"A Study in Scarlet"

24. Who owned and operated the St. Charles Speedway? His family has a road named for them.

Mel Hemsath

RABBITT'S TRIVIA GAME

In Our Town

★ ROUND THREE ★

1. Yesteryear architect Frank T. Hilliker, one of the founders of the Landmarks Association, was noted for only wearing ties with a certain design pattern. What was it?

Plaid

2. What's the name of the 2nd-floor event space at the one-time malt house of the Joseph Schnaider Brewery property at 2017 Chouteau Ave.?

Moulin Events & Meetings

3. What city in Ireland is a St. Louis Sister City?

Galway

4. The Soulard branch of the St. Louis Public Library was the work of what notable St. Louis architect?

Louis Spiering

5. What bank co-sponsors the annual St. Louis Jazz Festival, which takes place in Clayton?

U. S. Bank

6. The Adler Lofts, at 2035 Washington Ave., is named for a long-term first-floor business at that location. In what business was Adler engaged?

Picture framing

7. What high school is adjacent to the August A. Busch Memorial Conservation Area?

Francis Howell

8. Name the company that operates the Gateway Arch Riverboats.

Metro

9. Who was the Missouri Governor who committed suicide by shooting himself at his office in the Governor's mansion?

Gov. Thomas Reynolds (2/9/1844)

10. In the MGM movie *Seven Brides for Seven Brothers*, a St. Louis-born performer was one of the featured dancers. What's her name?

Virginia Gibson

11. What business did Cardinals baseball star Curt Flood operate at 5611 Delmar Blvd.?

Curt Flood's Gigi Room (a tea room)

12. Who is the internationally known operatic soprano who hails from Grand Tower, IL? She started her career in the Opera Theatre chorus.

Christine Brewer

13. What St. Louis Cardinals vice president is in the University City High School Hall of Fame?

Marty Hendin

14. What was the opening show at The Muny in 2004?

Meet Me in St. Louis

15. The 1932 book, *America As Americans See It*, edited by Fred J. Ringel, was intended to inform the people of Europe about life in the U. S.. What St. Louis native was listed as being known and admired by Europeans?

Josephine Baker

16. "Pointe 400" is the name for the luxury apartment project that now occupies the Pet Building at 400 S. 4th St. In stories, how tall is that building?

15 stories

17. What number designates the new runway at Lambert International Airport?

Runway 11-29

18. The building on the SW corner of 4th and St. Charles Streets, razed in early 2006 for a six-story office building, was used for what purpose?

The Federal Reserve Bank of St. Louis parking garage

19. For nearly 25 years, from the mid-teens to the end of the 1930s, one of St. Louis' leading local authors was Patience Worth. What made her unusual?

She was reputedly the spirit of a 17th-century Puritan who dictated her works to local resident Pearl Curran.

20. What was the first rail line to run a narrow-gauge train, with a portion of the tracks below the limestone bluffs of south St. Louis along the Mississippi?

Iron Mountain Railroad

21. Name the civic improvement organization that uses the slogan: "Building an Urban Village on the Edge of Downtown."

Old North St. Louis Restoration Group

22. The building at 1803 Pine St., currently the Salvation Army's Railton Residence and previously the Evangeline Residence, was originally the Robert E. Lee Hotel. What was it called between the time of its being the Robert E. Lee and the Evangeline Residence?

The Auditorium Hotel

23. The telephone exchanges ULrick and TIlden were used for what suburb?

Oakville

24. How many ballots did it take for Bruce Sutter to gain election to the Baseball Hall of Fame?

13 ballots

25. In what organization's former building, at 812 Union Ave., was The Little Theatre of St. Louis located?

The St. Louis Artist's Guild

26. Harry Swanger is the executive director of what musical group?

The Compton Heights Concert Band

27. The late Jack Buck became a member of what Hall of Fame in 2006?

The Hall of Famous Missourians (in Jefferson City)

28. In the late 1950s, Southwestern Bell offered telephones in 10 colors: Rose Pink, Aqua Blue, Light Beige, Moss Green, White, Cherry Red, Pastel Yellow, Light Gray, Ivory and one other color. What was it?

Black

29. What's the name of the association of St. Louis-owned and operated restaurants?

Saint Louis Originals

30. Over the years there have been 11 radio stations with studios in Clayton. Here's the list…minus one: KWUR, KFUO-AM &FM, KSLQ, KXLW, KLTH, KXOK, KXOK-FM, WEW, KADI. Which one is missing?

KRCH (it became KSLQ)

31. Upon his retirement, who replaced Dr. Glen Holt as Executive Director of the St. Louis Public Library?

Waller McGuire

32. What brand of beer did Anheuser-Busch introduce in 1998? It used a bird in its logo.

Catalina Blonde

33. What historic St. Louis building was developer Don Breckenridge planning to restore at the time of his death?

Kiel Opera House

34. The Zoo's famed Phil the Gorilla succumbed in what year?

1958

35. What was the street address of the first Busch Stadium?

3623 Dodier Ave.

36. Who was the founder of the St. Louis Veterans Day Parade and Observance?

Col. William S. (Bill) Lill

37. Name the local candy store chain that had a location at 524 N. Grand Blvd., directly across from the Fox Theatre.

Mavrakos

38. Prior to Vince Schoemehl's becoming Mayor of St. Louis, what Ward did he represent?

28th Ward

39. What one-time host of the "Today Show" on NBC was a graduate of University City High School?

Dave Garroway

40. "Wasn't I lucky to be born in my favorite city?" is a line from what movie?

1944's "Meet Me in St. Louis" from MGM

41. What former DJ of many years was elected Mayor of Maplewood?

Mark Langston

42. In an attempt to boost beer sales and promote beer in general, Anheuser-Busch created an industry development advertising campaign. What's the campaign called?

"Here's to Beer"

43. What's the name of the system of trails and parks proposed to connect Forest Park to Creve Coeur Park?

Centennial Greenway

44. What local rock bandleader (who's still performing) had the Teen-Tones and the Twist-Tones?

Jules Blattner

45. What was the name of the firm that had artsy architect Philip Johnson create their somewhat curious HQ building?

General American Life Insurance Co.

46. In the 20th century, the Cardinals won the pennant as National League champs several times. What was the second year for them to win this honor?

1928

47. What was the principal slogan for Joe Edwards' Rock 'n Roll beer?

"I sold my soul for Rock 'n Roll"

48. Famed 19th century and early 20th century restaurateur Tony Faust was born in what country?

Prussia

49. What's the name of the Internet smooth jazz radio station based in St. Louis?

The Vox

50. Name the actress whom Cardinals shortstop David Eckstein married in November 2005.

Ashley Drane

51. In round numbers, how many billions did Federated Department Stores pay for the May Department stores?

$11 billion

52. The broadcasting tower in the 500 block of DeBaliviere was not always at that location. Where in St. Louis was it originally located?

Between the 3600 block of Lindell and W. Pine Blvds., at the current site of the Pope Pius XII Memorial Library on the campus of St. Louis University

53. There's a Johnny Rabbitt Special at several dining spots in St. Louis, including Ted Drewes Frozen Custard stands. What is the Rabbitt Ted Drewes Special?

Johnny Rabbitt Chocolate Covered Cherry Concrete

MEMORIES 1947

The Beginning of Promtime

THIS IS A WORD SNAPSHOT OF THE ERA IN WHICH JULIAN MILLER created and nurtured Prom, a publication that was like none other in St. Louis, the U.S.A. or anywhere else for that matter. Arguably, Prom magazine may be the reason that folks then and now, some 60 years since Prom came into being, always seem to ask: "Where'd you go to high school?" Well, where did you go to high school? Just mention Prom or your school's name and a flood of magical memories pour into your thoughts.

Let's pay a visit to the past. To 1947.

The magazine rack by the lunch counter at Art Montgomery's Cut Rate Drug Store, 3136 Easton, is where, once a month on Wednesday, you'll find a bunch of kids from Vashon on Laclede, Sumner on Cottage and Washington Tech on St. Ferdinand snapping up that hot-off-the-presses new publication called *Prom*. It's even a hit with older students from Stowe Teacher's College on Pendleton, as well as kids from L'Ouverture grade school on Papin. Art's is a great gathering spot, as it's right by the Regal movie house (currently screening a double feature with Herb Jefferies, *The Bronze Buckaroo*.) This particular location is also good a place as any to chow down on chitterlings and a bottle of Nu-Grape from the ice water-filled soda box, as well as to get hep to what the typical St. Louis young Negro feels about the future, made promisingly brighter in these post-war days.

Getting a take on what white kids think about future times is easy to come by – say, over a cherry phosphate at places like the soda fountain at E. J. Stark, Jr.'s, E.J.'s Rexall Pharmacy in Maplewood, at 7300 Manchester, or at the fountain in that same community at Harper's Drug Store, 2818 Sutton (one of Tex Benecke's old hangouts). The *Prom* delivery from Pierce News would always make that day's after-school time more exciting, as the Maplewood-Richmond Heights High crowd would have something to chew the fat over, what with their very own column that at that time was also being perused by high-schoolers all over town.

Prom gives us a feeling of belonging and is as important to us as the Green-Stripe final edition of the *Star-Times*, a 5 Star copy of the *Globe-Democrat*, or the latest *Collier's*, *Look*, *Life* or *Police Gazette* is to our parents. And being a magazine, *Prom* pages stayed put, unlike those of the three daily papers, the pages of which are hard to control on the soda fountain counter, what with the wind whipped up by oscillating and ceiling fans. Over at the cigar counter, the chitchat of those over 21 seems oft to be about getting a better place in which to live in the far-off suburbs that were starting to blossom, beckoning families who wanted somethin' roomier, without pull-chain toilets and iceboxes. You could get a breezeway, picture windows, radiant heating and maybe a driveway and garage for the family "machine," which even the not-too-well-heeled are getting hold of as fast as they come off the line at the Chevy/Fisher Body plant on Union and Natural Bridge across from Uncle Dick Slack's furniture store. Chevy is an after-high-school job destination for many a guy from all over, but especially those from the not-too-far-off institutions such as Central on N. Garrison, Beaumont on Natural Bridge, Wellston on Wells, McBride on N. Kingshighway, Normandy on the Rock Road and Soldan-Blewett on Union.

According to the ads in *Prom*, there are plenty of other places for secure employment, such as Stix, Baer & Fuller, Boatmen's Bank, Southwestern Bell, Union Electric, Magic Chef, Scruggs, Boyd's and Laclede Gas – all places where you can work your way up through the ranks and eventually retire in a day way too far off to conceptualize.

Then, like now, if guys aren't dreamin' about gals – and vice-versa – they're longingly looking in showroom windows of car dealers, such as Otto Neupert's Studebaker agency on Southwest, not far from Southwest High; P.W. White's Nash showroom at 3116 Locust on the old automobile row, walking distance from Hadley Tech on Bell; Eddie Miller's Hudson agency at 1936 S. Vandeventer in Roosevelt's district; Weber De Soto-Plymouth, at 4035 Lindell, a couple of miles from St. Louis U High; or Willys-American at 4601 Delmar, where Army Jeeps were selling well. It's just a short streetcar ride from the Delmar Loop, the haven for University City High kids. You can imagine yourself behind the wheel of a sleek sedan or, better yet, in a rag-top, heading off to the Manchester drive-in movie, Parkmoor on DeBaliviere or to prom night at the Gold Room of the Jefferson Hotel. The latter event, of course, would be documented for all to see in an upcoming edition of *Prom*, with a Queen crowned by a favorite radio DJ, such as KWK's Rush Hughes.

Subdivisions are being planned as far west as Lindbergh (who in their right mind would want to move that far out?) and new homes, flats, duplexes and apartments are going up in the city at places like St. Louis Hills by Francis Park; just west of Clifton Park around Southwest Avenue; south of Carondelet Park to River Des Peres; and at "The Circle" in the Baden area.

It seems lots of us might be changing schools before long, but thanks to *Prom* we'll be able to keep up with our old pals. As we wait for whatever may come to be, we're happy with things like the newfangled ballpoint pens that seem destined to do in Skrip bottled ink and the blotter business; the return of the Chris-Craft speedboat; easy-to-get film for our Brownie camera; Southwestern Bell circuits, which were often tied up during the war but are now clear; going from a four- to a two-party phone line, and this thing called FM radio that offers crisp, clear sound without static if you can come up with the cash or credit for a new receiver. All the radios advertised in *Prom*, such as Capeheart and Motorola, are all AM only. Plus we'll need some good FM radio stations to listen to, and then maybe these FM radios will get hot. About all we've got now are stations like WIL, the first FM station in St. Louis, which signed on in '46, and KSLH, the Public Schools station, which only operates during school hours. But more are on the horizon.

The *Globe-Democrat* is building a big studio complex at 1215 Cole for their soon-to-sign on KWGD, but for now I'm okedoke with morning shows, such as Lee Adams on KMOX, the Shady Valley Boys on KWK, Don McNeil & The Breakfast Club on KXOK and Grandpappy Jones on WEW. Middays, there are soap operas like "Ma Perkins," "Young Dr. Malone," "Our Gal Sunday," "Big Sister," "Perry Mason," "Portia Faces Life," "Front Page Farrell," "Valiant Lady," "Guy Runion," "Aunt Jenny," and shows such as "Queen For A Day," "Morton Downey," "Superman," and "Ladies Be Seated." My favorite afternoon 78-rpm platter shows are hosted by D.J.s (or is it Dee Jays?) M.J.B., Rush Hughes, Del King or Bob Baker, and I'll dial around for national news from Cedric Foster, Ray Dady, Fulton Lewis, Jr., Alex Drier, Morgan Beatty, Edwin C. Hill, H. V. Kaltenborn, Gabriel Heatter and John B. Kennedy. Local news stories come from folks like Lindley Hines on KMOX and Frank Eschen on KSD. *Prom* publisher Julian Miller is trying to talk Chet Thomas, general manager of KXOK, the *Star-Times* station at 12th and Delmar, into having an hour show a week for *Prom* magazine (unfortunately it wouldn't happen). Then, before he pitched the idea to other outlets, Julian had second thoughts, as he was concerned that if you get could *Prom* over the air for free... why buy it? Plus, if the station carried advertising during the program, the money would go to them and not *Prom*...so *Prom* stayed in print and off the air.

After the homework and the dishes are done, there's plenty of evening entertainment on the airwaves, such as "Lum and Abner," "Big Town," "The Falcon," "Lux Presents Hollywood," "The Saint," "Counter-Spy," "The FBI in Peace and War," "Inner Sanctum Mysteries," "The Man Called X," "One Man's Family," "Fibber McGee and Molly," "Your Hit Parade," "Truth or Consequences," "The Great Gildersleeve," or maybe a Browns game broadcast on both WIL and WTMV. After the 10 o'clock news, with our *Prom* magazine on the nightstand, we fall asleep to programs from "Charlie Chan" to "Dizzy Dean" and musical segments with the Joe Shirmer Trio, Blue Barron, Harry James, The 3 Suns, Freddie Martin, Wayne King, and Ted Weems — with our own Russ Carter as song stylist. Many of these shows are broadcast from hotels like the Roosevelt in New Orleans, the Pennsylvania in New York and our very own Chase, owned by Sam Koplar and his son Harold. The 9th floor of the Chase was home for a time to KWK (and later WIL), and that great inn would become the address of *Prom*, Julian Miller and many of the countless *Prom* parties that would go on through the mid-80s (even though the magazine ended its long run in '73). But that's another story.

Television, with our *Post-Dispatch* station KSD Channel 5, is just getting started and causing quite a stir. But as far as I'm concerned, radio is just fine and so is *Prom* magazine. *Prom's* one of the best things to come along since V-J Day. And what a great time to be growing up. No war, no draft, we don't need red ration points for meat anymore or need to buy re-capped tires, the O.P.A. is history, oleo has color, war stamps and bonds and scrap drives are history, there are no more brown-outs, our Harry's in the White House and the United Nations is keeping the peace. Plus, just this month I was a S.N.I.P. (See Name In *Prom*).

Things could be worse ain't it?

RABBITT'S TRIVIA GAME

Be a Good Sport

★ ROUND FOUR ★

1. In 1997, who led the major leagues in homers while playing for an American League team, then for a National League team?

   Mark McGwire

2. Name the star player of the hapless '51 Browns who had the best batting average on the team and was a 20-game winner?

   Ned Garvey. He won 20 and lost 12 games while attaining a batting average of .305.

3. What newspaper writer's column was called "The Benchwarmer?"

   Bob Burnes

4. Red Schoendienst took over as manager of the Cards in '65. Who'd he replace?

   Johnny Keane

5. What school won the title as the 1959 basketball champs of the Suburban League?

   Webster Groves Statesmen. In the same year, the Public League champs were the Beaumont Blue Jackets.

6. What was the name of the St. Louis NHL team in the 1930s?

   St. Louis Eagles. They played at the Winter Garden on DeBaliviere Avenue.

7. There were four rules displayed on a sign in the old Busch Stadium batting cage. They were: 1. No drinks of any nature. 2. No food or candy. 3. No chewing tobacco. What was the 4th?

   No sunflower seeds

8. Before Joe Buck started in the announcing booth for the Cardinals on KMOX and on Fox Sports Net, he spent two seasons doing play-by-play for what team?

Louisville Redbirds

9. Who was the last owner of the St. Louis Browns?

Bill Veeck

10. What was the name of the East-Side sports facility at 6700 Missouri Avenue and Pocket Road?

Cahokia Downs Race Track

11. Rams owner Georgia Frontiere attended what St. Louis elementary school?

Hamilton, at 5851 Westminster Place

12. In 1956, what player did the St. Louis Hawks trade for Ed MacCauley and Cliff Hagen of the Boston Celtics?

Bill Russell

13. On what day did the wrecking ball actually strike our previous Busch Stadium to start the demolition project?

November 17th, 2005

14. Pitcher Urban Shocker won 20 or more games for four years in succession for the St. Louis Browns. In what decade did these feats occur?

The 1920s. He was 20 and 10 in '20; 27 and 12 in '21; 24 and 17 in '22; and 20 and 12 in '23.

15. In November of '62, when demolition started on the buildings that would make way for our second Busch Stadium, who was Mayor of St. Louis?

Raymond R. Tucker

16. For what benefactor is the Forest Park public golf course and clubhouse named?

Norman K. Probstein

17. When midget Eddie Gaedel played in a Browns game against the Tigers, what number did he wear?

1/8

18. In the mid-60s, what was the name of the Chicago Blackhawks' minor league team that played here at the Arena?

Braves

19. What St. Louis Football Cardinals running back and place kicker had a son who also played pro football? He was with the Cleveland Browns and other teams.

Terry Metcalfe. His son's name is Eric.

20. Name the architectural firm that designed the new Busch Stadium.

HOK Sport, a Kansas City-based division of St. Louis' Hellmuth, Obata + Kassabaum

21. Name the Cardinals pitcher who threw two no hitters during his Redbird career?

Bob Forsch – in '78 & '83

22. Who was the second African American to be signed to the St. Louis Browns?

Willard Brown, on July 19th, 1947. Hank Thompson had been signed two days earlier.

23. From the early 1950s until it closed, what three major league teams used Sportsman's Park/Busch Stadium as their home field?

Browns; baseball and football Cardinals

24. Who was the St. Louis Hawks player to become the first pro basketball player in history to score 20,000 points?

Bob Petit (forward), in 1964

25. What was the name of the colorful Cardinals public address announcer in the 1930s who was nicknamed "Fire Alarm" because of his penchant for chasing after fires?

Jim Kelly. He used a megaphone to make the announcements.

26. How many bases did the Cardinals (nicknamed "The Rabbits") steal during their 1985 pennant-winning year?

313

27. "Babe" Martin played for the Brownies in '44, '45 and '46, then again in '53. What were his actual first and last names?

Boris Martinovich

28. Who threw out the first pitch in the July 12th, 1966 All Star Game at Busch Stadium?

Vice President Hubert H. Humphrey

29. The Cardinals played one of the more unusual double-headers in history in '51, playing a day game with one team and a night game with another. What teams did the Cards play?

They beat the New York Giants 6-4 under the sun and lost to the Boston Braves 2-0 under the lights.

30. In another unusual double-header, this time between the Cards and the Cubs, the teams made a trade in the break between games. Cliff Heathcote played the first game as a Cardinal then the second as a Cub, and vice-versa for Max Flack. This odd occurrence took place on the 30th of May in what year?

1922

31. In '56, '57 and most of '58, the Cards were managed by Fred Hutchinson. He was fired with 10 games to go in his last year. Who replaced him?

Coach Stan Hack. His record for the remainder of the season was 3-7.

32. What Cardinals player crashed into the left-field wall in a 1962 game and had to be carried from the field?

Minnie Minoso. His full name is Satornino Orestes Armas Minosos Arrieta.

33. Who was the second African-American player to play for the Cardinals?

Willie Greason. The first was Tom Alston. They both came to the club in '54.

34. In what year did the Bidwill Boys move the football Cardinals to St. Louis from Chicago?

1960

RABBITT'S TRIVIA GAME

Eat, Drink & Be Happy!

★ ROUND FIVE ★

1. The name of the Catfish & Crystal dining room of Miss Hullings cafeteria at 11th and Locust Streets was borrowed from the title of a 1960 book by what author?

Ernest Kirschten

2. Beffa Brothers Buffet, which can trace its St. Louis roots to 1880 with a location in the Garfield House hotel on Market Street, has held forth on the south side of Olive Street at Beaumont Avenue since what year?

1898

3. What South Grand Boulevard restaurant was created by the late attorney and pediatric dentist Dr. Richard Parmeley?

Mangia Italiano, at 3145 S. Grand Boulevard

4. What was the last restaurant to operate in the Parc Frontenac apartment building at 40 N. Kinghighway Boulevard?

Nantucket Cove

5. Name the restaurant that immediately preceded Pizzeria della Piazza at 5100 Daggett Avenue.

Favio's. Others who served at that site included Galli's, Galimberti's and Cassani's.

6. Aumon's Tea Room, Europa 390, the Sideline Bar, the Women's Exchange, Alice B. Toklas, the Warfield Tea Room, El Rancho Buffet, Jacob Katz' deli, Hasty House, Habs House and the Hungry House were all, at various points in time, on what street?

N. Euclid Avenue

7. In what restaurant/bar/music club on Delmar will you see a holographic image of the owner when you walk in the front door?

Blueberry Hill

8. What St. Louis-based restaurant chain opened a location on the campus of St. Louis University? A co-owner of this company is on the university's board of trustees.

The Pasta House Company

9. Who created and operated the Jefferson Avenue Boarding House restaurant at 3265 Jefferson Avenue?

Chef Richard Perry

10. From 1975 into 1982, Bruce Sommer, of St. Louis Convention Center fame, operated a restaurant in an historic building at 911 N. Tucker Boulevard. What was it called?

The Sommer House

11. Carlos Berger left his culinary position at Harold Koplar's Chase Park Plaza to open what CWE dining spot? The location had once housed Bistro New Orleans, a Creole cuisine establishment.

The Red Brick at 101 N. Euclid Avenue, in the basement of the Parkedge Apartment Hotel.

12. The restaurant Savor occupies a building at 4356 Lindell Boulevard that was once a business operated by Saville Mayer. In what business was Mayer engaged?

He was a funeral director.

13. For many years, starting in 1953, Luigi's was noted for their original St. Louis-style, thin-crust pizza served at the four Luigi's eateries. Name the Italian restaurant that now occupies the first of those locations.

Lo Russo's, at 3121 Watson Road

14. A restaurant name with a heritage dating to 1812 returned in 2006 after having been absent for many years. It came back as a ground-floor operation in the 705 Olive building. Name it.

Teutenberg's

15. On November 9th, 2005, the original-recipe Luigi's pizza came back on the local restaurant scene. In what dining establishment is this classic pizza served?

At Meglio's Italian Grill and Bar at 12490 St. Charles Rock Road, owned by John Luca Meglio, nephew of Luca (Luigi) Meglio, who created the Luigi pizza pie

16. The Back Porch in Grant Fork IL (population 250) is an upscale, Florida- style, outdoor restaurant on the enlarged back porch of a family-style chicken dinner house. What's the name of the chicken place? It opened in 1892.

Diamond Mineral Springs. It's on Illinois 160, six miles north of Highland.

17. What was the name of the "Recommended by Duncan Hines" restaurant noted for home-style food such as baked chicken and hot biscuits with apple butter? It was at 606 N. Kingshighway Boulevard in the George Washington Hotel. (Later it was in the 4900 block of Delmar Boulevard.)

Mrs. Yoest's Hitching Post

18. What was the name of the market that preceded Adriana's at 5101 Shaw Avenue?

Rumbolo's

19. What grocery store chain once had locations in Northland Shopping Center, Crestwood Shopping Center and Brentwood Square? The chain remains in operation.

Straub's

20. In what dining establishment does The Magic Roundtable, a group of magicians, meet each Saturday afternoon?

Garavelli's cafeteria, 6600 Chippewa Street

21. Who was the noted wrestler who for several years operated The Chariton restaurant at 4301 S. Broadway? The Chariton, which had opened in 1928, was well known for barbecued meats.

Joe Tangaro

22. New Drover's Olde English Inn was in what community?

Fairmont City, IL, at the St. Louis National Stockyards Company

23. Name the independent benevolent organization that conducts weekly Wednesday lunch meetings at various restaurants. Members include Sheriff Jim Murphy; Lemay Fire Chief Neil Svetanics; Greg Rhomberg of the Antique Warehouse; Ron Battelle of The Back Stoppers; Mehlville Fire Chief Jim Silvernail; Airport Commissioner Joe Vacarro; Fox 2's John Pertzborn; retired Creve Coeur Fire Chief Bill Biele; Chuck Conners (announcer for the Jerry Springer Show); plus some 30 other members.

Greater St. Louis Public Affairs Alliance

24. There's the Duck Room music room at Blueberry Hill, but in what private club will you find The Duck Room dining room?

The Racquet Club, at 476 N. Kingshighway Boulevard

25. LeGrand's is a grocery and deli in St. Louis Hills, at 4414 Donovan Avenue. What was the previous name of this store?

Binder's Tom-Boy

26. What was the name of the 24-hour "greasy spoon" by the white water tower on E. Grand Avenue that featured brain sandwiches?

Pete's Hole In The Wall

27. Name the restaurant at 6923 W. Florissant Avenue that promoted char-broiled steaks "With a Reputation."

Zimmerman's Famous Village Inn & Coach Room

28. What firm owns the Bevo Mill restaurant?

Anheuser-Busch

29. What was the name of David Slay's first restaurant?

Café Hamton at 2607 Hampton Avenue. The building had housed a Dairy Queen and a Chicken Delight.

30. What's the name of the Illinois community that was originally called "Jersey Landing?"

Elsah

31. What was the full name of The Cottage restaurant that long ago was in Forest Park?

Schweickhordt's Cottage

32. Seven days a week, scrambled brains and eggs are served at what CWE restaurant?

The Majestic, at 4900 Laclede Avenue

33. What was the name of the restaurant at 100 W. Broadway, just across Eads Bridge in E. St. Louis?

Bush's Steak House

34. What are Soozie's Doozies?

Gourmet cookies that are made in Ellisville. Straub's is one of their outlets.

35. At what casino can you dine at the Captain's Table Buffet?

Argosy Casino

36. Al Solis, owner of the Mexican eatery Pueblo Solis at 5127 Hampton Avenue, also operates what bar-b-q restaurant?

Smokin' Al's, at 1216 Hampton Avenue

37. For more than four decades, Howard Mallot has been a manager for what St. Louis restaurant family?

Schneithorst's

38. For well over half a century, what game was played regularly behind the building that is now home of Lorenzo's restaurant, at 1933 Edwards Avenue?

Bocce. The place was originally Spezia's but is likely best remembered as John & Rose's.

39. What classy West County Italian dining house changed its name at the strong suggestion of a Las Vegas casino?

Café Bellagio. It's now IL Bellagio.

40. What's the name of the restaurant in Shaw's Garden?

Sassafras

41. What restaurant did Mary Hostetter open in 1985?

The Blue Owl in Kimmswick

42. On what street was the first Imo's pizza parlor located?

Thurman Avenue just south of 4100 Shaw Boulevard, which today is the location of the Imo's-owned Roma Baking Co.

43. Wade DeWoskin's Port St. Louis, late of Clayton, was first located on what street?

4283 Olive Street, in Gaslight Square

44. St. Louisan Larry Levy, of Chicago's successful Levy Restaurant operation, has finally brought his magic to St. Louis on Maryland Plaza, thanks to Ted and Sam Koplar. It's terrific to see the pizzazz of the late Harold Koplar and Sam Koplar in action again in the Central West End. In what business was Larry Levy's father, Paul, engaged in St. Louis?

Levy Novelty Co., and later L&R Distributing. These were phonograph record, jukebox and coin-operated novelty companies.

45. In the early '90s, what was the name of the night club in the Ramada Inn at Six Flags? They used the slogan "Where you're the star."

Flick's

46. What's the name of the book written about Crown Candy Kitchen, at 1401 St. Louis Avenue?

Sweetness Preserved

47. Name the O'Connell's Pub employee who started at the original Gaslight Square location, at 454 N. Boyle Avenue, more than 40 years ago. She was a character in the production "Gaslight Square," The Musical.

Norah McDermott

48. Al and Mary Baker are best known for their snazzy Al Baker's restaurant, at 8101 Clayton Road. (The Linens 'n Things parking lot is there today). What was the name of their preceding place on the DeBaliviere Strip?

Sorrento's restaurant and cocktail lounge, at 341 DeBaliviere Avenue

49. The Magic Pan crêperie had two locations here. One was at Plaza Frontenac, but in what shopping center was the second restaurant?

Northwest Plaza

50. What was the name of the cafeteria at 307 N. 7th Street, directly across from Famous-Barr?

The Forum

51. Since Cunetto's House of Pasta at 5453 Magnolia Avenue opened in 1974, they've always had the same chef. What's his name?

Charlie (Flipper) Sanfilippo. He came to them from Rich & Charlie's Trattoria.

RABBITT'S TRIVIA GAME

Gone – but (Hopefully) Not Forgotten

★ ROUND SIX ★

1. What was the name of the large meat-packing company complex in the City of St. Louis that was bounded on the south by N. Florissant Street, just east of Salisbury Street? The buildings and giant sign are still there.

Krey

2. "Steer to Bilgere" was the slogan of a Chevrolet agency that was located on what north-side street? Bilgere is gone, but the building remains.

N. Grand Boulevard (2820)

3. What was the name of the multi-story credit furniture store located on the SE corner of 11th and Olive Streets? It would later merge with a large home furnishing firm a block west at 12th Street (now Tucker Boulevard). Both buildings are long gone, the latter being destroyed by a major fire.

Carson's. They merged with Union-May-Stern to become Carson-Union-May-Stern.

4. Wiepert's was a 24-hour place downtown at the SW corner of 9th and Pine Streets. What type business was it?

Drugstore – specifically, a Nyal drug store. Until the late 1960s it was the ONLY 24-hour drugstore/pharmacy in the St. Louis area. The one-story building in which it was housed is just a memory.

5. What was the full name of the St. Louisan who wrote *The Glass Menagerie?*

Thomas Lanier (Tennessee) Williams

6. Hal Fredericks, Jack Elliott, Davey O'Donnell, Don "Stinky" Shafer, Ken Reed, Mort Crowley, David D. Rodgers, Bob Shea and Ed Bonner were all at one time affiliated with what radio station?

KXOK 630 AM

7. On what street was the Fairy Theatre located?

5640 Easton Avenue (now Dr. Martin Luther King Drive) at Blackstone Avenue. At last look, the building and its one-time adjacent airdrome were still there. It hasn't been used as a theatre since the early 1950s.

8. What was the family name associated with the 20th Century Market chain? They had stores in the Delmar Loop, S. 39th Street, DeMun Avenue and S. Grand Boulevard.

Schenberg – the stores were called "Schenberg's 20th Century Super Markets"

9. At what midtown intersection was the Melbourne Hotel located? It was home to the Kangaroom coffee shop and the Picadilly cocktail lounge. The building is still there and in use.

The Melbourne, which was an Albert Pick hotel, was in the building at the NW corner of Grand and Lindell Boulevards. It became Rogers Hall, a girls' dorm for St. Louis U, and now it's Jesuit Hall, a residence for priests.

10. What was the last City of St. Louis amusement park to close?

Chain of Rocks, at 10783 Lookaway Drive

11. In the 1964 production of *Show Boat* at the Muny, who played Cap'n Andy?

Andy Devine

12. The Scruggs-Vandervoort-Barney department store went out of business in 1968. At that time they had a downtown store, a branch in Clayton, another at Crestwood Plaza – and in what other shopping center was S-V-B located?

Northwest Plaza

13. Who was elected Governor of Missouri in 1960?

John M. Dalton

14. What was the name of the movie filmed in St. Louis in 1959 and directed by Charles Guggenheim?

The Great St. Louis Bank Robbery

15. When the Vincent Price 3-D thriller *House of Wax* played in May of '53 at the Fox theatre, what was the charge for the 3-D glasses needed to view the film?

15 cents. Including this with the ticket price, plus tax, adults got in for 90 cents. It was half a buck for kids, even thought the ads warned that they didn't recommend the movie for children.

16. In what city is President Ulysses S. Grant buried?

New York City

17. On what street was the Opera House located in St. Charles?

N. Main Street

18. What street bordered the west side of Sportsman's Park?

Spring Avenue

19. What was the major local news story of February 10th, 1959?

The tornado that struck the St. Louis area that day

20. What was the name of the amusement park that was located where Natural Bridge Road ended at St. Charles Rock Road?

Westlake Park

21. Which of the following did NOT have fried chicken as their specialty: Green Parrot, Buckingham's, Southern Aire, Grand Inn, Big Boy's, Pilot House or Lemmon's.

Grand Inn, at 910 N. Grand Boulevard, across from the V.A. Hospital. It was a Cantonese restaurant.

22. In 1998, what airline used the slogan: "We want to be your airline?"

TWA

23. In what building was Bruno's Bat Cave located? This was in the late '60s.

It was in the basement of George Edick's Club Imperial, on Goodfellow Boulevard and W. Florissant Avenue.

24. What number did Roger Maris wear as a St. Louis Cardinal?

9

25. At what Metro East park will you find a retired jet fighter plane on display?

Wilson Park in Granite City

26. David Surkamp (who's still going strong) was the lead singer for what band in the mid '70s? At the time they landed a contract with Columbia Records.

Pavlov's Dog (And I thank them for putting me on their liner notes.)

27. What was the name of Chuck Berry's nightclub on N. Grand Boulevard at Enright Avenue?

Club Bandstand

28. Who was the St. Louis mayor-to-be who operated a rhumba club in Hollywood during 1940-1941?

A.J. Cervantes. It was Alfonso Cervantes' Rhumba Club at the Bamba Club.

29. During the last years of his life, reputed St. Louis mob boss Tony "G" Giardano lived on what southwest St. Louis street?

In the 5800 block of Finkman Avenue in St. Louis Hills

30. What was the date of the great St. Louis storm of 2006?

The evening of Wednesday, July 19th

MEMORIES

The Airwaves

RADIO WARS: There's always been a battle for bucks in the radio biz, but today there are more stations than ever desperately seeking "the listener loyal." The goal is to create and market programming that will snag and retain the interest of the audience for big (and bigger) Arbitron ratings and, ultimately, for that almighty dollar to feed the coffers and shareholders of the national conglomerates, who these days operate most of the strongest signals of our 50-plus area terrestrial stations. In addition to iPods and satellite radio, these stations are starting to get competition from Internet outlets, owned in some instances by the same folks operating on AM and FM.

Time was, say in '59, that our town's radio ownership was mostly a hometown thing, with the exception of KMOX 1120 k.c. and KMOX-FM 103.3 m.h., which were owned and operated by CBS, then called the Columbia Broadcasting System. In '59, these stations moved from 9th & Sidney Streets in Soulard to state-of-the-art digs in the 1100 block of Hampton Avenue (now part of the Salvation Army office complex). It would be the first building put up by a network exclusively for radio since before WWII. Some of that station's stars were Rex Davis, Jim Butler, John "The Man Who Walks & Talks at Midnight" McCormick and Harry Caray.

KSD 550 k.c. had been in the St. Louis *Post-Dispatch* building at 12th & Olive Streets before the *Post* moved to the St. Louis *Globe-Democrat* building at 700 N. 12th Street. The radio station and KSD-TV moved next door, to 1111 Olive Street, in the area that had been used by the presses for the *Post*. These stations were owned, and had always been owned, by the benevolent Pulitzer family, who also delivered the afternoon *Post-Dispatch* to us. Passersby at that latter location could, on occasion, before the windows were blocked, get glimpses of personalities such as Frank Eschen, Russ David, Charlotte Peters, Ernie "Parade of Magic" Hellman, Russ "St. Louis Hop" Carter, Gil Newsome, Marty Bronson and Stan Kann.

We had KWK 1380 k.c., "The Personality Station," at 1215 Cole Street, in a building that had been erected in '47 for the short-lived KWGD, an FM station way before "the time" of FM. That Cole Street address is now best known as home of KDNL Channel 30, but it had been the site of our first Channel 4 station, KWK-TV. It, too, was a haven for those who liked to ogle local celebs, as it was where you'd regularly find folks of such fame as Ed Wilson, Jack & Jerry, Tom "Recall It & Win" Daily, King Richard and Les Carmichael.

KXOK 630 k.c. was a leftover asset of the defunct afternoon St. Louis *Star-Times* paper, which was steamrolled out of circulation by the *Post* in '51. Elzey Roberts, Jr., whose family made their big bundle in the shoe industry (Roberts, Rand, Johnson Shoe Co., which became International Shoe), was still the big stockholder, while others, including KXOK general manager Chet Thomas, held minority stakes. Chet, a true radio pioneer, started at the helm of 630 k.c. in 1936, when it was the dial location of KFRU, a 1,000-watt station in Columbia, Missouri, owned by the Roberts family.

KXOK signed on September 19, 1938, at 1250 k.c., in snazzy, Art Moderne studios in the *Star-Times* Building, at what was 12th Street and Delmar Boulevard (now the St. Patrick Center HQ). At the company's behest, the Federal Communications Commission soon allowed the stations to switch dial positions. Thomas ran the Columbia, MO, station until he was summoned to the big city by Elzey Roberts the elder just after the Japanese attack at Pearl Harbor. At that juncture, Chet was assigned to be Program Director of KXOK Tuesdays through Fridays and remain as General Manager of KFRU Saturdays through Mondays. In January '43, Thomas was made General Manager of KXOK, a position he held for 21 years. Roberts sold the station to Todd Storz of Omaha, heir to the Storz Brewing fortune, in late '61. Thomas, who is due much credit for his broadcast creativity over the years, stayed on as manager until he ankled in April 1964 to partner with Bob Stolz in the ad game, with newly formed Stolz Advertising.

In '56, KXOK had moved to a rambling, multi-level facility at 1600 N. Kingshighway Memorial Boulevard, across from Sherman Park, cattycorner from McBride High School and a block south of the Parkmoor. The property was a block long on Kingshighway and included five adjoined buildings. It was by far the largest facility for a radio station in St. Louis history. Some of KXOK's luminaries of the fifties were Bill Crable, Peter Martin, Bruce "Cloud Club" Hayward, Ed "Tops in Pops" Bonner, Buddy MacGregor and Rush Hughes, who had moved over from KWK.

In '59, WIL 1430 k.c. had been in the Coronado Hotel, at Lindell Boulevard and Spring Avenue, for a few years, having departed the 9th floor of the Chase Hotel, once home to KWK. That space was snapped up by Frank Block Advertising. WIL first occupied the area in the Coronado that had been The Jug restaurant and cocktail lounge, with its fountained, stone and marble, lower-level patio entry. That indoor/outdoor area is now home to Joe Boccardi's restaurant (where by the way, you can get a Johnny Rabbitt Special pizza). They quickly expanded to the west end of the first and second floor of the hotel as well.

Even though they moved in September '65, much remained of the way the studios looked as the facility was used for years by St. Louis University for its then KBIL, carrier current, student-run station (now KSLU). Then the studios sat silent and ghostly for all the years that the Coronado lay dormant. Since the rebirth of the hotel under the guidance of Amy and Amrit Gill, no vestige of a radio station remains at the Coronado.

In the fifties, if you wandered into the hotel's lobby (now restored to its original grandeur) or to the basement Coal Hole cocktail lounge at the east end of the building, you'd frequently run across station stars, such as Jack Carney, Bob Osborne, Dick Kent, Gary Owens, Ray Manning, Gene Chase, Dick Clayton or Reed Farrell, who'd frequently be with some of the hottest recording stars of the times as they were being wined by a local or national record or song plugger.

We also had Harry Eidlemann's KCFM, the first stereo station in town, at 532 DeBaliviere Avenue, in what had been a Food Center supermarket. There was WAMV, once WTMV, "The Voice of the Mississippi Valley," on the mezzanine of the Broadview Hotel in East St. Louis (home of the famous Sunday smorgasbord). WEW was on N. 4th Street, having moved from the American Hotel when that inn, and the theatre therein, were razed. There was KATZ, on the 3rd floor of the Arcade Building at 812 Olive Street; KXLW at 8614 Manchester Road; KADY on Highway 94 N. in St. Charles; KSTL at 999 S. 6th Street, with studios in Illinois; KFUO-AM and -FM, on the campus of Concordia Seminary; and the St. Louis Public Schools' station, KSLH, in the school building at 1517 S. Theresa Avenue. This station signed off for summer vacations and holidays and generally broadcast from 9:00 a.m. to noon (off for lunch) and then 1:00 to 3:00 p.m., Monday through Friday only. The FCC forced them to extend their hours years later.

If you'd like to delve into more of St. Louis radio & TV's past, we suggest a visit to the Library and Archives of the Missouri Historical Society, at 225 S. Skinker Boulevard. This institution houses a collection of thousands of items related to area broadcasting and has a full-time media curator in Klara Foeller. As founding president of the advisory board for this archive, I can say with certainty that the institution is always interested in collecting additional materials related to the field. Dr. Robert Archibald, president of the MHS, has taken a strong interest in the preservation of our radio and television history.

The St. Louis Public Library also maintains a considerable collection of media and St. Louis history, created under the direction of retired Executive Director Dr. Glen Holt and supervised by Jean Gosebink. And the St. Louis Mercantile Library Association, directed by John Neal Hoover, also houses a major media collection, especially in the area of the newspaper industry.

If you have any materials to donate to these institutions, or if you have questions regarding St. Louis radio and television history, feel free to contact me at this e-mail address: rabbitt@realoldies1430.com, or through Virginia Publishing.

RABBITT'S TRIVIA GAME

Somewhere There's Music

★ ROUND SEVEN ★

1. Ragtime pianist Trebor Tichenor is a nationally known collector of what type of musical "memorabilia?"

Piano rolls

2. What's the name of the notable record store that for decades was owned by Roy and Dorothy Gleason? (You do remember records?)

Webster Records (Dan Warner took over from the Gleasons, then sold the shop to Jennifer Bellm.)

3. What St. Louis rock & roll guitarist once played with Rod Stewart's back-up band?

Billy (Can A White Boy Play The Blues) Peek

4. Name the St. Louis Cardinals football star who is an accomplished singer and can occasionally be found vocalizing at public performances.

Jackie Smith

5. What was the name of the now defunct University of Missouri-St. Louis classical music series of many years that was founded and directed by the late Virginia Edwards?

Premier Performances

6. Entertainers Clea Bradford, Ceil Clayton, Marty Bronson, Davey "Nose" Bold, Singleton Palmer, Barbara Fairchild and many others were signed to what local record label?

Norman Records

7. Dale Benz is the veteran director of operations of what venue?

The Sheldon Concert Hall

8. Who is the big band leader and singer who gained national acclaim in the '40s and '50s and who, at the time this book was written, was still, at age 94, hosting a weekly jazz/big band radio show on WSIE, the Southern Illinois University at Edwardsville station?

Buddy Moreno

9. What was the name of the promising St. Louis rock group that in 1969 recorded a very Beatles-sounding album titled "Resurrection" at the Abbey Road Studios in London? They were signed to EMI for the Parlophone label but, because of problems within the group, EMI dropped them before the album was released.

Aerovons

10. Name the nationally successful Webster Groves-based record label owned by Richard McDonnell.

MAXJAZZ

11. Who's the nightclub owner and concert promoter who heads up the Fabulous Motown Review?

Steve Schankman

12. In the movie *Porgy and Bess,* whose singing voice is heard in place of that of Harry Belafonte?

St. Louisan Robert McFerrin

13. Name the transplanted New Yorker who started her St. Louis singing career on Gaslight Square. She received a Grammy for a commercial, has played The Muny on many occasions, and was honored for her body of work by the Missouri Historical Society's "Ragtime to Rock & Roll" exhibition.

Jeanne Trevor

14. What concert promotion company sponsored The Beatles' appearance at Busch Stadium?

Regal Sports (headed by Everett Agnew, Tom Agnew, Jr., and several others)

15. Country singer Barbara Fairchild was a grad of what high school?

McKinley

16. Name this star. He was raised in St. Louis, attended Washington U as a business administration major, won an Emmy in '79 as Best Supporting Actor and was awarded the Emmy for Best Actor in '85. He starred in the Los Angeles production of *Phantom of the Opera* for eight months. Who is he?

Robert Guillaume

17. Who was the legendary international singer, dancer, and comedienne who was born "Freda McDonald" in the Mill Creek Valley area of St. Louis June 3rd, 1906?

Josephine Baker (Her full name was Freda Josephine McDonald – she adopted her second husband's last name.)

18. Local Jazz musician Dave Venn is best known for playing what instrument?

Piano

19. What's the most recorded song written by Fran Landesman and Tommy Wolf of Crystal Palace fame?

"Spring Will Really Hang You Up The Most"

20. Two of Miles Davis' albums were live recordings made at what West End nightspot?

Jazz Villa, at Skinker and Delmar Boulevards

21. What was the name of the 1960s-era blues, R&B and jazz nightclub at 4300 Missouri Avenue in E. St. Louis owned by the late Leo Goodun? They featured live entertainment and a late-night radio show on KATZ that was first hosted by Spider Burks, then by Bernie Hayes.

The Blue Note Club

22. What was the name of the 1983 black gospel movie shot in St. Louis? Among others, it featured Mother Willie Mae Ford Smith and the O'Neal Twins.

"Say Amen Somebody"

23. One-time Mercury Records country artist Nick Nixon was in what profession before he became a full-time musician?

Optometry (He worked for Browne & Sanner Optometrists in the Humboldt Building at Grand and Washington Boulevards.)

24. What was the name of the first concert promotion firm to bring underground/psychedelic acts to St. Louis? They produced Cream, Steppenwolf, Iron Butterfly, Jeff Beck, Three Dog Night, Judy Collins, Procol Harum and many more.

Concert Productions. The firm was operated by attorney Jim Raymond and record promoters Dave Swengros, Mike Gratz and yours truly.

25. Which St. Louis rapper had a national hit with "Wat Da Hook Gon Be?"

Murphy Lee

26. "Kilimanjaro" was the name of one of the albums released by a group that frequently played The Dark Side (of the Moon) at 4210 Gaslight Square (Olive St.). They were originally on Norman records, then signed with Decca for national distribution. What is the group's name?

Quartette Tres Bien

27. In this chapter we've made several mentions of Norman Records, which was likely St. Louis' most prolific label of the last half of the 20th century. For whom was Norman Records named?

Norman Weinstroer. (He had been with Coral Records in New York, then opened Norman Record Distribution and Norman Records in St. Louis.)

28. In the '60s and '70s, many local, regional and national musicians bought gear from an exclusive music "shop" located above Tower Grove Music at Manchester Road and Tower Grove Avenue. What was its name?

Chuck Conners Professional Music

29. What DJ, on KXOK from 1962 until 1984, had previously been a singer signed to Stax Records of Memphis and had some success with radio play and sales in the south?

Nick Charles

30. What was Chuck Berry's only #1 pop hit on the Billboard Magazine charts?

"My Ding A Ling" in 1972

31. Name the country/western singer/musician who recorded for MGM, Columbia and Town and Country Records. He also played live radio shows, such as "Uncle Dick Slack's Big Old Fashioned Barn Dance" from the '30s to the '50s on KMOX with his partner, Frankie Taylor. Our mystery musician also had a role in the 1972 movie *Country Music on Broadway* and appeared many times on the Grand Ole Opry.

Clyde "Skeets" Yaney

32. What's the name of the local group that releases their recordings in French rather than English?

The Poor People of Paris

RABBITT'S TRIVIA GAME

On The Air

★ ROUND EIGHT ★

1. Who was the African-American disc jockey known as "The G?" He was long associated with KXLW.

George Logan

2. Name the male co-host of Channel 5's "Show Me St. Louis" who departed that show to take an around-the-world trip in the spring of 2006?

Chris Balish

3. Who's the former network TV talk host who sued the *National Enquirer* for $100 million bucks? She started her TV show locally on Channel 5 and also did a network radio show from KXOK. She lived on McPherson Ave.

Sally Jesse Raphael

4. Julius Hunter ankled TV4 to work for what institution?

St. Louis University

5. Who was Guy Phillips' original male co-host on KY98?

Mike Wall

6. When KMOX was in Soulard, on what street was it located?

Sidney Street

7. What church-based broadcaster owns 4 over-the-air stations and 2 Internet stations in St. Louis?

Bonneville International (The Mormon Church)

8. What was Dry Gulch George's last name? He was the announcer on "The Wrangler's Club with Texas Bruce" on Channel 5.

Abel

9. What radio station at various times had studios in the Melbourne Hotel, the Chase Hotel, the Coronado Hotel and the Centennial Building?

WIL

10. Name the former St. Louis firm that was the original occupant of the building on Market St. now used by KEZK and KY98? This company had been in the Brown Building on the SE corner of Tucker Boulevard (12th Street) and Washington Boulevard.

Eagle Stamp Co.

11. Who is the seven-time Emmy Award winner who is one of the owners of KTRS?

John Goodman

12. What major network St. Louis TV station does not have daily local news broadcasts?

KDNL (ABC)

13. Who is credited as having been the second DJ in St. Louis-area radio?

Bob Baker

14. What KSHE jock was nicknamed "The Musical Pumpkin?"

Lee Coffee

15. Name the radio station that actually had an Eskimo carve a totem pole as part of grand opening ceremonies at a new broadcast home.

KXOK --for Radio Park, 1600 N. Kingshighway Boulevard

16. Who was the radio traffic reporter who created the term "gaper block?"

Officer Don Miller

17. What DJ has a food item named in his honor at Fast Eddie's Bon Air in Alton?

Vic Porcelli of the station that was "The River." It's Vic's Chick On A Stick, which sells for $1.99.

18. When Buddy Blattner and Howie Williams broadcast St. Louis Browns baseball over KWGD-FM, what brewery was their sponsor?

Falstaff

19. What are the call letters of the TV station owned by the Rev. Larry Rice's New Life Evangelistic Center?

KNLC

20. Name the St. Louis-based Internet rock station that proclaims they play "the best independent artists from around the world?"

I-Channel

21. Richard King hosted the top rock and roll show on KWK Radio in the late '50s. What air name did he use?

King Richard

22. Broadcaster and entrepreneur John Craddock is best known as...?

Frank O. Pinion

23. What local DJ is "enshrined" in the Rock and Roll Hall of Fame in Cleveland?

Yours truly, Johnny Rabbitt

24. Which radio station got national attention in the 1950s for "breaking" all of their rock 'n roll records?

KWK 1380

25. Radio station KCFV is affiliated with what area educational institution?

St. Louis Community College District

26. Miss Blue, who was actually a cleaning lady, became a featured performer on whose radio show?

Jack Carney's, on KMOX

27. Who hosted the "St. Louis Hop" on KWK-TV 4?

Ed Wilson

28. Who hosted the KSD Channel 5 version of the "St. Louis Hop?"

Russ Carter

29. What radio station has been broadcasting and transmitting from the same facility since 1927?

KFUO, on the campus of Concordia Seminary in Clayton. The AM station started broadcasting in 1927, and the FM in 1948.

30. During September 2006, what station started using the slogan "Makes You Feel Good!"?

Movin' WMVN 101.1

31. What KWK (later KSD) radio star took possession of the first Corvette sold in St. Louis?

Gil Newsome

32. What long-time broadcaster's last regular on-air role was as host of the cable show "Seniorville?" He had been on KXOK and KMOX radio as well as KWK-TV and KTVI, where he anchored the 10 o'clock news.

Bruce Hayward

33. When Chuck Norman sold WGNU-FM to Doubleday Broadcasting, what call letters did the station adopt?

KWK-FM

34. In 1992, a St. Louis and Missouri Media Archive was started at what local institution?

The Missouri Historical Society

35. In 2006, what institution created a Media Halls of Fame display?

The St. Louis Mercantile Library Association

36. The first station to broadcast in stereo used the broadcast tower atop the old Boatman's Bank Building (now Marquette Condominiums) at 300 N. Broadway. What station was it?

KCFM

37. What radio station was part of a national Transit Radio Service and directed their programming to those riding streetcars and buses? They placed receivers (that picked up only their signal) and speakers on these conveyances.

KXOK-FM

38. St. Louis' first full-time jazz station signed on in the mid-1960s from studios in the Continental Building. What station was it?

KADI

39. WIL-FM morning hosts Cornbread and Pat came to St. Louis from what city?

Wichita (KFDI)

40. What former St. Louis television personality appeared on Johnny Carson's "Tonight Show" more frequently than any other guest?

Stan Kann

41. The interesting and creative Bruce Bradley broadcast over three stations in the St. Louis area during his career here – KMOX, KTRS, and what was the other?

WIBV, Belleville

42. Who replaced the late Jack Snow as master of ceremonies for the 10th annual ('06) Epilepsy Foundation Bowl-A-Rama at Tropicana Lanes?

Bernie Miklasz

43. At the end of his testimonial commercials, what 1950s DJ used the tag line "tell 'em E.B. sent me?"

Ed Bonner on KXOK

44. Who was the Channel 4 weatherman who was also a noted jazz DJ?

Jim Bolen

45. In what year did Ted Koplar's World Events Productions introduce the now hotter-than-ever TV character "Voltron?" The original Voltron episodes are now available on DVD.

1984

46. At what radio/television-related organization is Molly Hyland employed? Her dad was Robert Hyland, who was CBS Regional Vice President and head of KMOX-AM & FM (also called KHTR and later KLOU).

AFTRA – The American Federation of Television and Radio Artists

47. At the height of his broadcast career at KXLW, the late Spider Burks was proclaimed in the newspapers as "being the highest paid negro" in St. Louis. Within $5,000, what was his salary?

$20,000

48. In what apartment building was KPLR-TV originally located?

The Chase Apartment, 4931 Lindell Blvd.

49. When Classic 99 KFUO's Jim Connett was a DJ on WRTH 590 AM in the 1980s, what was his theme song?

"Classical Gas" by Mason Williams (possibly prophetic)

50. Who hosted the "Night of a Thousand Stars – First Run Theatre" movie series on KMOX-TV 4?

Thom Lewis

51. Who played the roles of "Hiram & Sneeb" on KTVI Channel 2?

Jack Murdoch and Harry Honig

52. When I was Johnny Rabbitt on KXOK, who was my original "sidekick?"

Harvey the Hare

53. Who was the jazz jock known as "The Man in the Red Vest?"

Leo Chears

54. What station uses the slogan "Radio Free St. Louis?"

WGNU

55. In June '06, Tim Albright, morning show producer for WVRV, left to take the job of Director of Media Operations for the radio and TV stations at Lewis and Clark College in Godfrey, IL. Who hosted that morning show?(They were the last morning hosts for that station).

Steve & DC

56. Name the radio personality and educator who published the 2006 book, *The Death of Black Radio – A Personal Perspective of Black Radio?*

Bernie Hayes

57. The Veiled Prophet parade was broadcast for the first time in 1925. On what station was this aired?

KSD

58. WIL-AM 1430 has its transmitter and towers in Dupo, IL. What's the name of the road on which this facility is located?

WIL Road

59. Former sports broadcaster Buddy Blattner was a world champion in what sport?

Table tennis (ping pong)

60. What brand of beer was Harry Caray pictured in the newspapers as drinking following his dismissal by Anheuser-Busch?

Schlitz

61. There are two 50,000-watt AM stations in the St. Louis market. One is KMOX 1120. What is the other?

KXEN 1010

62. The self-supported broadcast tower near the NW corner of Hanley Road and Brentwood Boulevard was constructed in the 1980s for what radio station?

KADI

63. "Percy Dovetonsils" was a nickname given by Jack Carney to what KMOX newscaster?

Rex Davis

64. Former TV news broadcaster Dennis Riggs is director of what cable station?

HEC – Higher Education Channel

65. For a period of time in the 1950s, who was the KMOX female late-night host?

Lou Payne

66. What firm sponsored the locally produced dramatic series "The Land We Live In?" It aired from 1942 to 1953 over various stations.

Union Electric

67. In 2005, who was honored with the annual Bob Hardy Award for support of our armed services? This award is part of the Veterans Day Parade and Observance held at the St. Louis Soldiers Memorial Military Museum.

Craig Cornett of KSD-FM. (His wife received the award in his name, as he had departed St. Louis for a short tenure in Atlanta.)

68. What St. Louis radio station was first to broadcast in HD?

KFUO-AM 850

69. In 1960s radio, Ron Lipe became better known by what air name?

Prince Knight on KSHE

70. Who is the former TV weather lady who is a spokesperson representing Mayor Francis G. Slay?

Dianne White

71. At what establishment in St. Louis is there a tribute to Skeets Yaney in the form of a recreated studio used by the country DJ?

Jasper's Radio Museum and Tropical Fruit Baskets. It's at Cherokee Street and Illinois Avenue.

72. KMOX's Ron Jacober was once an owner of what Illinois radio station?

WINU, Highland, IL

73. Comic DJs Ron & Joy are best recalled here for their work on KSHE. What are their "on air" last names?

Ron Stevens & Joy Grdnic. Today they operate a successful radio syndication service out of St. Louis called "All Star Radio Networks."

74. In what building was KMOX located in 1929?

Merchants Exchange, at 3rd and Pine Streets

75. What were the call letters of the St. Louis Public Schools radio station?

KSLH. It was located at 1517 S. Theresa Avenue.

76. In 1954, what network was attempting to win the license to broadcast on VHF station Channel 11?

The Columbia Broadcasting System. Of the four other applicants, 220 Television would be the winner. This group was headed by the Koplar family. "220," by the way, is the address of the then Koplar-owned Park Plaza Hotel.

77. For some time, the "Cityscape" show on KWMU was hosted by Mike Sampson, who passed away. Don Marsh did the hosting honors temporarily. Who is the permanent host of that show?

Stephen Potter

78. KRSH Radio is operated by what school?

Ritenour High School

RABBITT TRIVIA GAME

Parks

★ ROUND NINE ★

1. What was the fuel source used to provide electricity for the 1904 Worlds Fair? Was it oil, wood, coal, solar or natural gas?

Coal

2. On what building will you find a painting of the Apotheosis of St. Louis? The image was accidentally reversed when it was painted.

Sheraton City Center Hotel & Edison Condominiums

3. What city park is named in honor of a man who was both mayor of St. Louis and governor of Missouri?

Francis Park (David R. Francis)

4. What city park is adjacent to what had been Potter's Field?

Tilles Park

5. St. Louis Zoo director Marlin Perkins came here from what zoo?

Chicago's Lincoln Park Zoo

6. A major outdoor display at the World's Fair was a clock in front of the Palace of Agriculture. The face was 118 feet in diameter. Of what material was the clock made?

Flowers

7. What's the name of the Zoo's bug exhibit?

Insectarium

8. In actual acreage, what's the 2nd biggest park in the City of St. Louis' park system?

River Des Peres Park

9. What was the name of the section of the World's Fair in which would you have found infant incubators, the Magic Whirlpool, the Hereafter, the Battle Abbey, the Galveston Flood and the Spectatorium?

The Pike

10. In what city park will you find the Frank T. Hilliker Memorial Bridge?

Carondelet

11. On what street is Strodtman Park located? It was donated to the city in 1924 by businessman George Strodtman in honor of his wife Genevieve.

Palm Street, between 13th and 14th Streets

12. Name the first public park in the St. Louis area on the west side of the Mississippi River. It opened in 1812.

Dakota Park in Carondelet

13. What's the name of the park bounded by 13th and 14th Streets, Locust and St. Charles Streets?

Lucas Park

14. The ghosts of Confederate soldiers reportedly haunt a local park in which they were executed? Which park is it?

Lafayette

15. Who gave the name Thornhill to the house and property that's now part of West County's Faust Park?

Missouri's second governor, Frederick Bates

16.In what area park will you find the largest assemblage of the art work of St. Louisan Ernest Trova?

Laumeier Sculpture Park

MEMORIES

★ 1969 ★

TIME-TRAVEL WRITERS OFTEN SUGGEST THAT, TO AID A SOJOURNER in returning to the past, it might help to find an environment in which time has seemingly stopped. No easy task. But let's give it a shot and try to resurrect some ghostly gastronomical glimpses of 1969 as we seek the way it was on the St. Louis dining and drinking scene.

You might consider voyaging back from a booth at the Karandzieffs' never-changing Crown Candy Kitchen at N. 14th and St. Louis in Old North St. Louis as you dreamily put away a Johnny Rabbitt Special malt and reminisce with some '69 songs on the jukebox, such as: "Get Back" or "Yesterday" by the Beatles, Stevie Wonder's "Yester-Me, Yester-You," or Zager & Evans' "In The Year 2525 (Exordium & Terminus)."

In no time at all, you'd feel as if it were 1969 all over again, and you could head out the door for such used-to-be spots as The Bismarck restaurant, operated by Steve Boianoff and Steve and Ivan Johnoff on N. 12th St., across from the Sheraton-Jefferson Hotel. You might snap up a bowl of their real (not mock) turtle soup and a chicken or crabmeat Coronado sandwich, which were their versions of the Prosperity. A true Prosperity was being served behind the stained glass windows over at the Hofbrau in the Mayfair Hotel, where Welsh Rarebit was also a specialty.

'Course your cruise could take you to a three-martini lunch at Jasper Bonventre's Rose's at 10th St. and Franklin Ave., where you'd rub elbows with princes of print from the *Globe* or *Post*. Rose's could trace its roots to Prohibition days, when it was Rosario's. Chef Joe Pugliese created some of the best Italian vittles in town, starting in 1943. But there's a twist to this tale. Rose's, which was demolished for the Convention Center, moved lock, stock and recipes to Giuseppe's on S. Grand and Meramec, where Mr. Joe took over the reins from Jasper over a quarter of a century past. Now Joe has sold, but the new owners still create his original recipes – sans pizza, which had been a Rose's menu favorite.

Another location where you could start your time trek would be Beffa Brothers' Buffet – if you can find it. Now, since Beffas' location is a carefully guarded secret, all I can tell you is that if you were to happen to find yourself at the intersection of Beaumont Ave. and Olive St., you'd be very, very close to the Beffa inner sanctum. Don't look for a sign; it isn't there. Don't use your cell phone to call information for the number, 'cause they don't have a listing. And if you happen to have a criss-cross street directory, forget it, they're not there. BUT if you open the correct door, you'll be in a place where the food and decor is much as it was back in '69. If you happen in on Tuesday, get a plate of beef stew. It'd make Dinty Moore hang his head in shame. On Wednesday, go for the green ham. But whatever day, Monday through Friday, you'll find something special that'll take you right to the then-that-was. Oh, don't ask for a menu. They don't have one...and there's no price list either.

From Beffas' you might wander off in search of a Flaming Pit, of which there were plenty, with more on the way in '69, as Harry Hilleary was signing up franchisees at a rate where The Pit seemed like it could be the new McDonald's. One location was at 6435 Chippewa St., in the same building that had housed the first Stan Musial and Biggies eatery.

Other '69 stops might be for a frosty draught of Stag beer at Charlie Blitt's Buffet, at the NW corner of Manchester and Tower Grove Avenues, with its landmark Stag neon sign. Or you could cross Tower Grove and pick up a six-pack of 9-0-5 beer from the package liquor store that bore that name. Nearby was Ulrich Brugger's café on Chouteau at Boyle Avenues, where the sandwich supreme was Braunschweiger with mustard on rye bread.

A '69 midtown Mecca for good eats, including freshly made pastries, was Norm, Norb and Dave Sewing's Salad Bowl cafeteria (and Bits & Saddles lounge) at 4057 Lindell Blvd. Elmer Sewing had started it off in the '40s on Lindell, just east of the Windsor Hotel, when it was, and remained, somewhat like a Miss Hullings west.

Of course, in '69, but no more, you could indulge in the myriad delicacies that the Miss Hullings cafeterias offered in the basement of the Chemical Building at 8th and Olive Streets and at 11th and Locust Streets. What chicken pot pies! What split lemon and chocolate cakes! What a job Steve Apted did in keeping the legend of Miss Hullings, His Lordships cocktail lounge and Catfish & Crystal restaurant (once the Grey Ghost) alive long after others would have given up the ghost. Ditto for La Sala, which served south-of-the-border vittles in the Executive building at 515 Olive Street.

If your time machine starts to run out of juice, jump on the elevator for the 6th floor of Famous-Barr (Macy's) and The St. Louis Room, which is eerily much the same now as then. You can taste the past with a bowl of that famed Famous French onion soup, which Henry Ettman, Jr., and Stanley Goodman's daughter, Ellen Goodman (Lowenstein), discovered in the late '50s in NYC at The Brasserie in the Seagrams Bldg.. They passed the word on the soup to Stanley, Famous-Barr's topper at the time (and dad to Ellen). You could also have been among the first to sample Chicago's Baskin-Robbins ice cream, which premiered here on the first floor at Famous downtown.

A near-sighted glance could make you think you could revisit Busch's Grove of '69, but that Clayton Rd. front is only a façade, like that of a movie set. But there are other portals to the past, such as the venerable Racquet Club at 467 N. Kingshighway Blvd.; Al's at 1st and Biddle Streets; Chuck-A-Burger on the Rock Road, across from Ritenour High; Cusanelli's on Lemay Ferry Rd.; Romine's on Riverview Blvd.; Ponticello's on Bellefontaine Rd. in Spanish Lake; Frank and Helen's on Olive St. in U. City; The Tenderloin Room in the Chase Park Plaza; Dooley's on 8th at Olive; Culpepper's on Euclid; The Fox and Hounds in the Cheshire Inn on Clayton Rd.; Failoni's on Manchester; the Mayfair Room at the Roberts' Mayfair Hotel; Goody-Goody on Natural Bridge;

Bevo Mill; the Majestic on Euclid; Monte Bello's Pizza on Weber; Rigazzi's on Daggett; Al Smith's on S. Grand; Ted Drewes on S. Grand or Chippewa; and Pietro's on Watson Rd.

Today the only way to visit the following, once notable eating and drinking establishments would be to master the mystical secrets of time travel and pay a visit to 1969: The Coffee Pot on Delmar and Skinker; Buck Horn Bar by the Continental Trailways station on N. Broadway; The Crest House at Broadway and Chestnut; Schneithorst's Big Bevo on Hampton; Little Bevo on Morganford; The Branding Iron on Meramec in Clayton; Frank Mormino's Europa 390 on N. Euclid; El Vesuvio on Watson (Rte. 66); Sloan's Blu-Top on Page; Grone's on Grand and Lafayette; Garavelli's on Olive west of Grand; Garavelli's on DeBaliviere; Sala's "Under the Viaduct" on Daggett; La Rocca's on Lindell; Rice Bowl Shangri-La on S. Grand; Mascara's on Chippewa at River Des Peres; Pagliacci's on Manchester and Kingshighway; The Tack Room at the Chase Park Plaza; Saro's Sunny Italy on Chippewa at Lansdowne; the Saum Hotel dining room on S. Grand; The Pelican on S. Grand and Shenandoah; the Peach Garden on Olive east of the Empress Theatre; The Parkmoor, either on Clayton and Big Bend, at Manchester and Lindbergh, or across from Ted Drewes on Chippewa; Dohack's on Lindbergh and Lemay Ferry; Ruggeri's on Edwards (with Stan Kann playing the organ); Carl Wethington's hot dog emporium on Hampton; Steiny's Inn on 66; Herman and Bernice Laub's Ranch House on Chippewa; Lombardo's on Riverview; the Playboy Club on Lindell; Cassani's on Daggett; and the Rex Café on Olive St. and Newstead Ave.

We could go on with a few hundred other places that have passed into the ever-dimming recesses of the past, but it's time for your 1960s trivia test. After you pass, maybe we can get together for lunch in a circa-sixties beanery.

RABBITT'S TRIVIA GAME

The Swingin' Sixties

★ ROUND TEN ★

1. In what year was Stan "The Man" Frank Musial elected to the Baseball Hall of Fame at Cooperstown, N.Y.?

    1969

2. What was the name of the legitimate-stage theatre in the Spanish Pavilion when it was rebuilt in St. Louis?

    Sir John Falstaff Theatre. The building is now part of the Hilton St. Louis at the Ball Park, formerly the Marriott Pavilion Hotel and originally the Breckenridge Pavilion Hotel.

3. What noted baseball player and broadcaster's brother was a ring announcer for "Wrestling at the Chase?" The events were staged at the Chase Park Plaza hotel under the auspices of promoter Sam Muchnick and were telecast on The Koplar family's KPLR Channel 11?

    Joe Garagiola

4. What brand of beer was brewed and bottled in St. Charles in the sixties?

    Van Dyke

5. What was the name of the Miss Hullings restaurant that opened in the Bel-Air East Hotel at 4th Street and Washington Avenue?

    Miss Hullings Open Hearth. The St. Louis Downtown Hampton Inn at the Gateway Arch is the current name of the hotel.

6. Who was "The Man Who Walked and Talked at Midnight" on KMOX Radio?

    John McCormick

7. What was the name of the public walkway that ran north and south between the 4200 blocks of Olive Street and Washington Boulevard? It was almost in the center of Olive's Gaslight Square and was between Jack Carl's Two Cents Plain and Monteleone's.

Washington Way

8. At the time Forest Park Highlands burned in 1963, what was the name of the ride just inside the main entrance on Oakland Avenue?

The Flying Turns

9. Who played Cap'n Andy in The Muny's 1964 production of *Show Boat?*

Andy Devine

10. What major St. Louis department store closed in the sixties? They had stores downtown, at Crestwood Plaza, Northwest Plaza and in Clayton.

Scruggs-Vandervoort-Barney

11. As we entered the '60s, what were the call letters of the television station located at 1215 Cole Street? It's now KDNL Channel 30.

KWK-TV Channel 4. It would become KMOX, then KMOV.

12. At the beginning of the '60s, on what street was the legitimate-stage American Theatre located?

N. Grand Boulevard. The address was 318. Immediately before the American moved there, it had been the Shubert. When the American moved, it became the Loew's Mid-City.

13. What drugstore chain, with eight locations, had a large store with a balcony at 700 Locust Street, in the 315 Locust Building? (The actual address of the building was 315 N. 7th Street.)

Katz Super Drug Stores

14. What was the name of the Bar B Q place at 21 Forsyth Walk in Clayton (between Forsyth Boulevard and Maryland Avenue)?

Sam's Chuck Wagon Bar B Q

15. What did KSD-TV Channel 5 weatherman Howard DeMere say at the end of his weathercasts?

"That's all from here, Howard DeMere."

16. Name the soft drink that sponsored the "Hi-Fi Club" on WIL Radio in the early '60s.

Coca-Cola

17. What was the name of a leading local furniture store chain with its main store and offices at 911 Washington Avenue?

Lammert's

18. The slogans "King Quality" and "None Better" were used by what business?

Quality Dairy at 4646 W. Florissant Avenue

19. Steppenwolf, Dionne Warwick, Melanie, James Brown, Incredible String Band and The Temptations were all presentations of Regal Sports and sponsored by what brand of beer?

Falstaff

20. At what theatre did the 1963 epic *Cleopatra,* starring Elizabeth Taylor, Richard Burton and Rex Harrison, have its first-run engagement in St. Louis?

The Ambassador at 7th and Locust Streets

21. In late 1960, what heavyweight boxer was warned by Senator Estes Kefauver, chairman of a Senate investigating committee, to discontinue his relationship with local mob boss John J. Vitale?

Charles "Sonny" Liston

22. What radio station for a time used the slogan "The Swinger?"

KADI, which was on the 15th floor of the Continental Building at 3615 Olive Street

23. For a time, Gaslight Square had a small movie theatre located in the Musical Arts building at 459 N. Boyle Ave. What was the theatre's name?

Gaslight Cinema

24. What St. Louis County Catholic high school opened in 1960?

St. John Vianney

25. What local architectural firm co-designed the 1962 Priory Chapel at 600 S. Mason Road?

Hellmuth, Obata & Kassabaum

26. What CWE bookstore was created by a group of Washington University undergraduate students in 1969?

Left Bank Books. Barry Leibman has owned it since 1977.

27. In what year did Alfonso J. Cervantes become Mayor of St. Louis?

1965

28. What nickname had been given the player who was traded for Joe Torre of the Atlanta Braves in 1969?

"El Birdo" – Orlando Cepeda

29. Likely the most flamboyant Sam Spade-style private eye of the era had his detective agency at 4229 Lindell Boulevard. He would speed through midtown and the CWE in a Corvette convertible and was quite the raconteur and character. He was found murdered, sitting in a truck. What was his name or the name of his agency?

John W. Murphy of the Murphy Detective Agency

30. In 1964, there were three Slay's restaurants in the area. There was one at 2652 Hampton Ave., which featured steaks and Lebanese cuisine, another at 10205 Gravois Road, with steaks and German dishes, and a third served Italian dishes and featured pizza. At what intersection was this third restaurant?

Manchester Road and Brentwood Boulevard – 8804 Manchester Road (Slay's Caruso's)

RABBITT'S TRIVIA GAME

Who, What, Where, When?

★ ROUND ELEVEN ★

1. Prior to St. Louis University's acquisition of the Cupples House mansion at 3673 W. Pine Boulevard, what union occupied that building?

    Order of Railroad Telegraphers

2. Name the original dining establishment at 3852 Lindell Boulevard. The location became Flaco's Tacos, then Crazy Bowls and Wraps.

    Toddle House

3. What was the name of the manufacturing firm at 2001 S. Hanley Road?

    Wallace Pencil Co.

4. What was the name of the department store at 8001 Forsyth Boulevard? Subsequent to the store's closing, the building retained the owner's name. That corner is now the site of a First Watch restaurant.

    Gutman Department Store

5. Who was the future mayor of the City of St. Louis who had his insurance company office at 3910 Lindell Boulevard?

    Al (A. J.) Cervantes

6. In what structure is the Aquatunnel located?

    The Climatron at Shaw's Garden

7. At what church will you find the local Beehive Clothing location?

    The St. Louis Temple of the Church of Jesus Christ of Latter Day Saints at 12555 N. 40 Drive

8. Name the major department store that had one of the three suburban branches of their downtown headquarters at the SW corner of Hanley Road and Forsyth Boulevard.

Scruggs-Vandervoort-Barney

9. What was the name of the restaurant on the top floor of the 7777s building at 7777 Bonhomme Avenue?

Top of the 7777s

10. What airport was located at Rudder Rd. and Highway 66 in St. Louis County?

Weiss Field

11. What was the name of the movie theatre at 4023 Olive Street?

Congress

12. The building in which the Record Exchange at Hampton Avenue and Eichelberger Street is located was built for what use?

The Buder branch of the St. Louis Public Library

13. Name the one-block city street that disappeared with the destruction of the Bannister Estate apartments buildings, between York and Euclid Avenues from Lindell Boulevard on the south to the alley on the north.

Argyle Place

14. What noted civic leader's brewery was destroyed by fire on November 3rd, 1829?

John Mullanphy's

15. A pair of weeping lion sculptures can be found at an entrance to what park?

The Grand Boulevard entrance to Tower Grove Park

16. On what street was the Door and Zeller Ice Cream and Catering Co. located? The building is still there.

401 DeBaliviere Avenue at Waterman Boulevard

17. In which direction is the statue of Thomas Jefferson in The History Museum building at Forest Park facing? Is he looking north, south, east or west?

North

18. In 1964, which was the tallest building in Clayton?

Pierre Laclede Building, at the NW corner of Hanley Road at Forsyth Boulevard

19. What "college" that taught "beauty culture" was located at 808 Washington Avenue?

The Moler System of Colleges, better known as the Moler Barber College

20. In what Gaslight Square restaurant was there a significant stained glass window depicting Romeo and Juliet?

The Three Fountains in the Musical Arts building, on the SW corner of Boyle Avenue and Gaslight Square (Olive Street)

21. What was the name of the "way" that ran from the 4000 block of McPherson Avenue to the 3900 block of Enright Avenue? It ran across Olive Street, Washington and Delmar Boulevards and was between Vandeventer and Spring Avenues.

Culver Way

22. At 5867 Delmar Boulevard (just east of the original Pageant Theatre), there was a renowned fried chicken eatery. What was it called?

Golden Fried Chicken Loaf

23. What was the original name of the hotel that became the Sheraton Clayton Plaza?

The Colony

24. Petite Pigalle was a French-themed restaurant in the basement of what CWE apartment hotel?

The Windsor, at 4209 Lindell Boulevard

25. John's Town Hall dining and drinking establishment is in the Dorchester apartments on Skinker Boulevard. On what street was the original Towne Hall located?

Clayton Road (6736)

MEMORIES

The Beatles Story

★ CHAPTER ONE ★

IT WAS IN LATE SUMMER '63 WHEN I HAD MY FIRST BEATLES ENCOUNTER. I was at KXOK Radio 630 in North St. Louis' Radio Park when I received a small pasteboard box in the mail that contained some foreign newspaper clippings and a few 45 rpm records from Europe, all performed by a strange-sounding group, unknown to me, called the Silver Beatles and the Beatles. The package, and handwritten note therein, had been sent by a doctor's wife, Louise Harrison Caldwell, who lived in Benton, Illinois. She said she was a regular listener of the Johnny Rabbitt Show and KXOK and explained that she was a sister of one of the band members.

Out of curiosity, we auditioned the songs, but had no intention of playing any records – no matter what they were like – that were not available for sale in the USA. To be honest, we didn't think much of the sound – or even the chances for the group to get an American company record contract. The only hit import acts during that year to date were "Sukiyaki" by Kyo Sakomoto and Rolf Harris' "Tie Me Kangaroo Down, Sport." Later in the year, "Dominique" was a top 10 song by The Singing Nun, and Los Indios Tabajaras made it big with "Maria Elena." NO songs from England made it to the American Top 100 in all of 1963.

We really thought we'd heard the last from Louise and her brother's band. Boy, were we wrong.

RABBITT'S TRIVIA GAME

Ride On!

★ ROUND TWELVE ★

1. Name the automobile dealer who was president of the St. Louis Cardinals for 28 years starting in 1920.

Sam Breadon

2. In what public room of the Chase Park Plaza Hotel will you find an artist's rendering of the most prominent cars made in St. Louis from the early '20s to the early '30s?

The Legacy Room, a memorabilia room in the Chase building

3. What make auto was assembled and sold by the Western Automobile Co. in the building complex on the southeast corner of Euclid Avenue and Washington Boulevard?

Pierce-Arrow

4. In December, 1907, the first automobile show was held in St. Louis. In what building did the event take place?

The Jai Alai building at 520 DeBaliviere Avenue – later the Winter Garden Ice Skating Rink

5. What make automobile was sold by the Gene Janzten dealership at 5434 Natural Bridge Avenue?

Chevrolet

6. Architect Preston J. Bradshaw is best known for the hotel and apartment buildings he designed. But his greatest concentration of work was for automobile agencies. On what street were these buildings located?

Locust St., known as "Automobile Row." Several of these structures are still standing.

7. The first Volvo dealership west of the Mississippi River opened in 1955 at 8500 Watson Road. What was the name of that agency?

Ed De Brecht Imported Cars., Ltd.

8. In 1959, Wright Motors, at 6111 Delmar Boulevard, was the only St. Louis County dealer selling a car billed as "the newest American automobile in over a generation." What make was it?

Edsel

9. In what year did the Ford Motors assembly plant open in Hazelwood?

1949

10. The first national auto parts distributor opened here in 1899. What was the name of this company?

A. L. Dyke Automobile Supply Co. In 1905, they moved to a building, still standing, on the west side of Walton Avenue between Olive Street and Washington Boulevard.

11. AAA is in a building at 3917 Lindell Boulevard that replaced a previous Auto Club building at that site. What was the last organization to occupy the old building before AAA?

Knights of Columbus

12. Who was the one time Rolls-Royce dealer on S. Kingshighway Boulevard?

Charles Schmitt

13. The world's first gas station opened here in 1905. On what street was it located?

S. Theresa Avenue. It's now the site of a grassy knoll between eastbound and westbound I-64/40, a block east of Grand Boulevard.

14. In the 1920s, a car called the "Locomobile" was sold from the building at 3033 Locust Street. Later, and for years, it was home to a famous film and recording studio. What was the name of the studio?

Premier Studios. During WWII, studio operator Wilson Dalzell was credited with cracking a Japanese espionage code broadcast over a St. Louis radio station by a hillbilly band.

15. Name the Pontiac dealer who used the slogan "Him heep big trader."

Charles E. Vincel Pontiac, at 3295 S. Kingshighway Boulevard

RABBITT'S TRIVIA GAME

See What You Know!

★ ROUND THIRTEEN ★

1. The final auction of slaves took place on the steps of the Courthouse (now the Old Courthouse) in what year?

1860

2. The Great Fire of 1849 started on the steamboat *White Cloud*. What was the name of the second boat to catch fire?

The Edward Bates

3. Henry Shaw's remains are in the mausoleum at the Missouri Botanical Garden, but what cemetery had Shaw originally selected as his final resting place?

Bellefontaine Cemetery

4. In 1877, David May, founder of the late, great May Co. Department stores, opened his first store in what city and state?

Leadville, Colorado

5. How many sections are there in the Gateway Arch?

142. The last section was put into place in October '65.

6. In what midtown building did then Senator Harry S Truman maintain an office?

The Masonic Temple at 3681 Lindell Boulevard. At the time, he was head of the Masonic order in Missouri. Incidentally, Truman was Time *magazine's Man of the Year for 1945 and was pictured on the cover of* Time*'s December 31st issue.*

7. The community of Meachum Park was named for what person?

Rev. John Berry Meachum. He was an African-American minister active in the Underground Railway movement.

8. Andrew Lloyd Weber's *Aida* played The Muny during the 2006 season. When did the original, operatic version of *Aida* play at that amphitheatre site?

1917. It was performed for the convention of the Advertising Clubs of the World.

9. What type structures did Henry Shaw visualize as being built on a 200-foot periphery around the entire Tower Grove Park property?

Italianate-style villas. Only one was built. It's the home of the park director and is at the SE corner of Magnolia and Tower Grove Avenues.

10. What name did Auguste Chouteau suggest for what would become the village of St. Louis?

Laclede's Village

11. Who won the U. S. Senatorial contest of 1852 between Stephen Douglas and Abraham Lincoln? During the campaign they engaged in seven debates, with the final one taking place in Alton on October 15th.

Stephen Douglas

12. In what park will you find the Sons of Rest Pavilion?

Tower Grove Park

13. In what year did the St. Louis State Hospital celebrate its centennial?

1969. It was originally named the St. Louis County Insane Asylum.

14. What was the name of the German "Song Circle," founded in 1870, that was for years located at 2163 S. Grand Boulevard, on the NW corner of Flad Avenue? It was razed for a Jack in the Box.

The Liederkranz Club

15. Eads Bridge, one of the most identifiable landmarks of America, was the creation of James B. Eads and was dedicated on July 4th, 1874. What was Eads' middle name?

Buchanan

16. Near what Illinois community will you find the Knobeloch State Nature Preserve?

Freeburg

17. The Dauphin Players is the name of the theatrical performers at what high school?

St. Louis University High

18. The George I. Barnett-designed stone house named "Oakland," at 7802 Genesta Street, was built in 1854 for what leading banker?

Louis Auguste Benoist. Barnett, then of Barnett & Peck, also designed the brick Tower Grove house for Henry Shaw in 1849. That house was stuccoed in 1919.

19. In what cemetery is Louis Auguste Benoist buried?

Calvary

20. Who is the native St. Louisan who played the role of Liesl Von Trapp in the 1964 Muny version of *The Sound of Music?* Also at The Muny, she had played Kim McAfee in *Bye Bye Birdie* in 1962 and Becky Thatcher in the 1960 production of *Tom Sawyer.* In Chicago she had her own television program called "Susan's Show."

Susan Heinkel

21. The St. Louis Fire Alarm Dispatch Center was first located in what building?

In an attic of the Old Courthouse

22. Who was the only white man to be killed by Indians in Franklin County? He resided in a one-room log cabin, built in 1804, in what would become Pacific.

John Ridehour. He was watering his horse when he met his fate at the hands of some Shawnee Indians.

23. What famous person lived at 4633 Westminster Place?

Tennessee Williams

24. At the turn of the 20th century, what was St. Louis' largest hotel? It opened in 1894.

The "new" Planters. It closed in 1922.

25. In 1955, these municipalities were located in what county? – Times Beach, Schuermann Heights, Arbor Terrace, Margona Village and Mary Ridge.

St. Louis County, which at the time had 96 municipalities

26. See if you can come within a dollar: What would it cost for a reserved seat to see a Cardinals game in 1951?

$1.85

27. Name the St. Louisan who has released several books in the "Images In America" Series. One of the titles is: *Central West End, a Pictorial History.*

Dr. Albert Montesi. The author is a retired St. Louis U. professor.

28. Former Edison Brothers honcho Eric Newman created a money museum that was housed in what downtown bank?

Mercantile

29. Which branch of the St. Louis Public Library is named for a late St. Louis educator whose extensive collection of African-American books, manuscripts and papers is housed in this library?

Dr. Julia Davis. The new Julia Davis Library opened in 1994 at 4415 Natural Bridge Avenue.

30. Name the famous downtown delicatessen that ceased operations in December 2005.

Jack Carl's Two Cents Plain, at 1114 Olive Street

MEMORIES

The Beatles Story

★ CHAPTER TWO ★

LOUISE HARRISON Caldwell, George Harrison's sister, wasn't satisfied with the initial rejection of her brother's band, The Beatles, by KXOK and by competing Top 40 station WIL. She made several phone calls to us and sent more press clippings from Europe, as well as additional copies of their records. The long hair of the band members was also a turnoff, as they looked so different from our clean-cut American hit makers, such as Bobby Vinton, the Beach Boys, Dion, Andy Williams, Steve Lawrence and Al Martino. Our Top 40 competitor, WIL, also told her they had no interest in The Beatles and no intention of playing them.

At that time there were no other stations in town playing rock 'n roll, as KWK had "broken" their rock records and KSHE was still four years away from becoming "Real Rock Radio." Louise continued to relentlessly pursue airplay at KXOK, more so than at WIL, as our broadcast signal was much stronger and she could hear us at her home in Southwestern Illinois. This was in the late summer of '63. I only wish I'd kept those European Beatles records she kept sending . . . they'd bring a small fortune now on e-Bay.

RABBITT'S TRIVIA GAME

Shaw's Garden

★ ROUND FOURTEEN ★

1. At the time Henry Shaw officially opened his public Garden on July 15th, 1859, was Shaw a citizen of England or of the United States?

United States. He became a citizen on July 3rd, 1843.

2. Name the New York architect who designed Henry Shaw's city house at 7th and Locust Streets, Tower Grove, his country home, and the museum building in the Garden.

George I. Barnett

3. Dr. George Englemann, a principal advisor to Henry Shaw on botany, was a specialist in what medical field?

He was a gynecologist.

4. In what St. Louis church did Henry Shaw's will arrange for a "Flower Sermon" to be held each May?

Christ Church Episcopal Cathedral

5. Who immediately preceded Dr. Peter Raven as director of the Missouri Botanical Garden?

Dr. David M. Gates, a physicist

6. Garden director Dr. Peter Raven was born in what country?

China

7. In what year did the Climatron open?

1960 (dedicated on 10/1, opened on 10/2)

8. What was the principal building replaced by the Climatron?

The Palm House

9. What type of dome is the Climatron?

Geodesic

10. One of the two principal St. Louis architects for the Climatron was Joseph D. Murphy. Who was the other?

Eugene J. Mackey

11. Which area of the Garden is called the "garden of pure, clear harmony and peace?"

The Japanese Garden, "Seiwa-en"

12. Name the City of St. Louis off-site division of Shaw's Garden.

EarthWays House on Grandel Square

13. What's the name of the Garden's annual Holiday Flower and Train show?

Gardenland Express

14. The Shaw Nature Reserve is in what community?

Gray Summit, MO

15. What was the original floor covering used in the first-floor hallway of Shaw's Tower Grove House, which was built in 1849?

Kamptulicon (similar to linoleum). Kamptulicon dates to 1843. Linoleum was patented in 1860.

16. Who became director of Shaw's Garden following Shaw's death?

Dr. William Trelease, who held a doctorate in science from Harvard

17. At what age did Henry Shaw retire from business?

39

18. Between 1819 and 1825, Henry Shaw spent the warmer months in St. Louis and wintered in another city. What city was it?

New Orleans

19. What was the original name of the restaurant in the Ridgway Center?

Gardenview

20. Name the United States president who proclaimed the Missouri Botanical Garden as "a great legacy to the people of Missouri, the United States, indeed the world."

President Ronald Reagan (June 12th, 1984)

21. Was Henry Shaw ever a slave owner?

Yes. He owned 11 slaves.

RABBITT'S TRIVIA GAME

Shopping in The Twilight Zone

★ ROUND FIFTEEN ★

1. "They Say the Sweetest Things" was a slogan for what candy company? Their candy plant at 4709 Delmar Boulevard supplied their dozen shops, including those in Crestwood Plaza and Northland Shopping Center.

Mavrakos

2. What was the name of the neighborhood department store at 2614 N. 14th Street, down the block from Crown Candy?

Sobel's Department Store. It made it into the '90s.

3. Name the Oldsmobile dealer at 10105 Manchester Road, at Sappington Road, circa 1960.

Nolting

4. What was the drugstore chain that offered delivery service by "The Boys in Red?" Even going back into the 1930s, they had a half-dozen stores, including one at Hanley Road and Wydown Boulevard in Clayton.

Glaser

5. There was a local ice cream store chain that at one time had four DOZEN retail stores. They had three in U. City alone, including one of their last locations at 630 North and South Boulevard. What was the chain?

Velvet Freeze (Their chocolate chip was the yummiest.)

6. What was the name of the ladies' shop at 8131 Maryland Avenue? It would later move to Plaza Frontenac.

Helen Wolff

7. Name the department store company that had stores at 9957 Manchester Road in Warson Woods and at the Village Square shopping center.

Golde's

8. If you were worn out from shopping, what restaurant on DeBaliviere offered curb service in 1926? (Car Lane or The Parkmoor is incorrect.)

Joe Garavelli's – on what was called "The Garavelli Corner" of DeBaliviere and DeGiverville Avenues

9. Who was known as "The King of Lamp Shades?" The King was in Maplewood. The company's still in business today.

Brody's

10. You'll need to gas up to keep shopping so you might pull into one of this local company's 10 stations. There's still a painted-over sign at their former location at 3325 Chouteau Avenue. What was the chain? Hint: It was named for a celestial body.

Mars

11. For decades you could have picked up a bauble at the jewelry store on the corner of 9th and Olive Streets (826 Olive Street) in the Paul Brown building. Name the store.

Hess & Culbertson

12. What was the name of the appliance store chain that took over Tipton?

Silo

13. 1010 Locust Street was the address of a famous furrier that started here in 1896. Do you remember?

Kessler

14. What was the men's store at 310 Westport Plaza?

Victorian House

15. In 1959, what was the largest locally owned grocery store chain in this area?

Bettendorf's, with 11 stores. Schnuck's had four and Dierberg's, one. In 1939, Jim Remley stores were tops, with six locations.

16. What was the name of the major printing business at 45 E. Lockwood in Webster Groves? It was destroyed by a massive conflagration in April, 2002.

Scholin Brothers Printing Company

17. The Vogue Boot Shop for ladies, which celebrated its 75th anniversary in 1996, was located on what downtown street?

It was last at 912 Olive Street. It had been at 615 Locust Street.

18. Speaking of shoes, many folks used to "Head for the Hills." What multi-store chain used that slogan? They were hot in the '50s and into the '60s.

Hill Brothers Self-Service Shoe Stores

19. What was the name of the four-story moving and storage company that for many years was at 1 S. Grand Boulevard? It was razed for the St. Louis U. parking garage at the corner of Laclede Avenue.

Frank C. Baker Storage & Moving Co. They offered steam heat and 500 separately locked storage rooms.

20. Who was the former Air Force photographic instructor who operated a well-known commercial photography business at 308 N. Theresa Ave. in midtown?

"Buzz" Taylor

21. There were two large, multi-location bakeries in N. St. Louis. One was Koob (which promoted their products with the slogan "Good Health-Good Food" and had six retail locations). What was the name of the other firm, which ran 10 stores?

William F. Ellerbrock

22. What was the name of the commercial dairy, which also had a dairy shop at 4455 Chippewa Street, just a little east of Famous-Barr Southtown?

Ozark Dairy

23. What railroad had a station under the overpass at Tower Grove and Vandeventer Avenues?

The Frisco Railway. The Missouri Pacific had a street-level station just down the street, at 1486 S. Vandeventer Avenue.

24. What was the name of the locally based, national dance studio that had several locations in St. Louis, starting just after WWII at the Roosevelt Hotel? They were also a block west of Famous-Barr Clayton at 7325 Forsyth Boulevard, 6000 Natural Bridge in the Terry Moore bowling alley building, and on the second floor of the Marina building at 306 N. Grand Boulevard at Lindell Boulevard.

Ray Quinlan Studios

25. In the mid-90s, we had a short-lived, all-business, news and information radio station. What were the station's call letters?

WCEO 590 AM. It was located at 7711 Carondelet Avenue in Clayton. Today it's KFNS, a sports station.

26. What was the name of the home furnishing store at 3601 W. Florissant Avenue, at E. Grand Avenue?

Ideal

27. Name the antique reproduction company that used to operate from the building that once housed the Crystal Palace on Gaslight Square, at 4240 Olive Street.

AA Importing Co. They're now at 7700 Hall Street.

28. Randy's Card Corner, which dealt with sports cards and collectibles, was located in what drug store?

Affton Drug, at 9440 Gravois Road

29. What department store was known as "The Grand-Leader?"

Stix, Baer & Fuller

30. In 1957, you might want to finish the day with a cool Tom Collins or a Cuba Libre at the cocktail lounge long located at 2606 N. Kingshighway Memorial Boulevard. It was across the street and just a block and a half away from DePaul Hospital. What was the name of the lounge?

The Corkscrew

MEMORIES

The Beatles Story

★ CHAPTER THREE ★

IT WAS SEPTEMBER '63. ONE OF THE BIG LOCAL NEWS STORIES THAT YEAR was that, as Steven B. Stevens, a KXOK newsman had reported, a conflagration had ended the life of our venerable and much-loved Forest Park Highlands. The good news in our country was that President John F. Kennedy had created a form of Camelot in America. We at KXOK were too busy playing and saluting the music of the good old USA – from the Beach Boys, Little Stevie Wonder, the Four Seasons and the Kingsmen – to pay any attention to music from England, let alone by this group of mop-haired unknowns who called themselves "The Beatles." But George Harrison's pesky sister kept after us.

So one night, to – we hoped – keep her quiet, we put a Beatles song on the Johnny Rabbitt Make It Or Break It segment. The song, as I recall, was "From Me to You," and it did pull a great number of calls. But more than 90% of those voting said to Break It! We really thought that was the end of The Beatles saga.

If only we had known then what we would know four months later.

RABBITT'S TRIVIA GAME

Triviamania

★ ROUND SIXTEEN ★

1. Name the lubricant cleaner (similar to WD-40) manufactured by a Clayton based company.

Alum-a-lub

2. SqWires restaurant is in a complex on S. 14th St. in Lafayette Square originally occupied by what firm? (Western Wire Manufacturing Co. is NOT the correct answer.)

American Bed Factory

3. Who was the SLU football coach when the St. Louis U Billikens threw the first legal pass in college football? It happened September 5th, 1906.

Eddie Cochems

4. The Grand Marais Golf Course in Metro East is located in what state park?

Frank Holten State Park

5. KETC Channel 9's street address is 3655 Olive St. What was the name of the car rental agency that occupied that site during the mid-20th century?

Heater Rent A Car & Truck Co.

6. In 2006, where did the James S. McDonnell USO open a branch site?

Ft. Leonard Wood

7. What family operated the Western Brewery Co.?

Lemp

8. What's the name of the radio reading service for the visually impaired operated by the Missionary Oblates of Mary Immaculate?

Minds Eye Information Services (It's broadcast on a sub-carrier signal of WMVN.)

9. In what city park will you find a bronze statue of George Washington? It's a copy of the marble statue sculpted by Jean Antoine Houdon?

Lafayette Park (It's been there since approximately 1869.)

10. The late movie star Shelley Winters once lived on what southside street?

De Tonty

11. What retail division of Brown Shoe Co. has the most locations nationwide?

Famous Footwear

12. In 1951, who was president of the St. Louis Browns?

Bill DeWitt

13. What area community has the most Lustron (metal) homes, which date from the late 1940s into 1950?

Webster Groves

14. Who was the Rams quarterback whose 1999 season was cut short by an injury?

Trent Green

15. Who is the famed St. Louis photographer whose talent was discovered as she frequently roller bladed her way through the Central West End snapping shots?

Suzy Gorman

16. The dome of the Old Courthouse is made of wrought iron and what other material?

Cast iron

17. What noted millinery shop opened in South St. Louis in 1915? It remained at the same location for more than 80 years.

Hat Mart (3411 California Ave.)

18. Who was the first postmaster of St. Louis?

Rufus Easton

19. What CWE private place was created by businessman Jacob Goldman? He named it for his deceased daughter.

Hortense Place

20. Name the retired firefighter used as the model for the St. Louis Firefighters Memorial Statue in Poelker Park across from City Hall.

Ralph Jones (He was a firefighter from 6/49 to 9/84.)

21. In 1948, a St. Louis company created a short-lived device that was marketed to teens to wear in their shoes. What was the name of the company?

Kliker. The devices would make the shoes emanate a "click-click" sound. They also came with silencers to wear in school.

22. What was the name of the early St. Louis fur company owned by the Chouteau brothers, Berthelemie Berthold and John Jacob Astor?

American Fur Co.

23. What is the full name of the Energizer battery company's Hall of Fame?

Energizer Keep Going Hall of Fame

24. In what building was the City of St. Louis Law Library located before it moved to the Civil Courts building in 1930? The building still exists, but it's now encompassed within a larger structure.

Pierce building. The west end of the Adam's Mark hotel is actually the Pierce building.

25. Name the Jesuit priest who wrote the book *The St. Louis Irish.*

Fr. William B. Faherty, S.J.

26. What was the name of the multi-decade cocktail haven at 409 N. 11th St., just north of Locust Street? It was part and parcel of the Miss Hullings operation.

His Lordship's

27. What internationally known actor once lived at 6320 Forsyth Blvd.?

Vincent Price

28. Who is the locally famed developer grandson of Byron W. Moser? Moser was president of Security National Bank and later Southern Commercial Bank.

Joe Edwards

29. R & F Macaroni (now Pasta) Co. was opened in St. Louis in 1901 by John Ravarino and Joseph Freschi. In what city is R & F made today?

Kansas City, MO

30. Once upon a fun time, the Racer Dip and Mountain Ride were part of what amusement park?

Forest Park Highlands. They'd later be the Flying Turns and The Comet.

31. In what business were the following establishments of the 1920s engaged: Ratz's, Hong Far Low, Cocksburger's, Chimney Corner, Roach's, Stiff's, Black Cat and Fong Yick's?

They were all restaurants.

32. What theatre was originally described as being of "Hindoo Temple" architecture?

The Fox

33. With what network was KPLR originally affiliated?

None. It was an independent station.

34. In June 1931, James M. McGinley received a U. S. Patent for what item?

The detachable support for the drive-in restaurant car window tray. It premiered here in 1931 at the McGinley-owned Parkmoor. The first, and last, location was on Clayton Rd. west of Big Bend Blvd.

35. What radio station is located in the building that for years housed the Barnabas Ficht bakery?

KDHX, at 3504 Magnolia Ave.

36. In what year did the ill-advised St. Louis Centre open?

1985. It shuttered as a shopping center in September 2006.

37. What was the original name of the University City Hall building?

The Magazine Building

38. The St. Louis University Museum of Art, in the 3600 block of Lindell Blvd., was originally home to what organization that is still in existence?

The St. Louis Club

39. What is the latest name for the DeBaliviere Place neighborhood?

Metropolis

40. What Hill neighborhood dining house is owned by Giovanni Galati?

Dominic's

41. With whom did Ozzie Smith compete for the Cardinals shortstop position in '96?

Royce Clayton

42. How many sculpted figures are there in the Carl Milles-designed fountain in Aloe Plaza? It was originally named "The Wedding of the Waters" and renamed "The Meeting of the Waters" to appease some prudes of the population.

14

43. Who was the Gardner Advertising ad executive who wrote and produced the radio serial "Tom Mix and His Ralston Straightshooters" for Gardner's client, the Ralston-Purina Co.? It was the longest-running and highest-rated children's program in radio history.

Charles E. Claggett, Sr. He passed away 1/8/98.

44. In which of the following mediums was local artist James Godwin Scott best known: oil, acrylic, pen and ink, watercolor, charcoal, pastels, or pencil?

Watercolor

45. What was the name of the bowling alley once partially owned by Stan Musial and Joe Garagiola?

Red Bird Lanes (It was located at 7339 Gravois Rd. for 33 years.)

46. Prior to Antoine Soulard's arrival in St. Louis, he had been a lieutenant in the Royal Navy of what country?

France. He fled the country to escape the guillotine.

47. Name the Chicago department store that's vacating a classic State Street structure designed by Louis Sullivan, the architect of our Wainwright building.

Carson Pirie Scott

48. What was the name of the long-time music school at 7801 Bonhomme Ave. in Clayton? It was razed, along with other structures, to make way for the Chromalloy building.

St. Louis Institute of Music

49. What television station originally occupied the studios that are now those of KTVI Channel 2?

KSTM Channel 36

50. Who had back-to-back wins of the U. S. Open and the Buick Classic golf tournaments in 1990?

Hale Irwin

51. In what principal field did the late Martin Quigley toil?

He was a writer.

RABBITT'S TRIVIA GAME

Past Times

★ ROUND SEVENTEEN ★

1. At the mouth of what river did Lewis and Clark first observe the Pacific Ocean?

Columbia River

2. In 1836, Sidney, Victor and Ann streets in Soulard were named after the children of the first mayor of St. Louis. What was his full name?

William Carr Lane

3. In what cemetery will you find the remains of both Dred Scott and Gen. William Tecumseh Sherman?

Calvary Cemetery

4. In 1949, a widow, Mrs. Carlton Hadley of St. Louis, announced that she would be marrying. Who was the nationally known groom-to-be?

Vice President Alben W. Barkley

5. Two devastating tornados struck St. Louis in the 20th century. The first was in 1927. On what exact date did the second occur?

February 10th, 1959

6. In his residence at what church was Fr. Edward Stanislaus Filipiak found murdered in 1979?

Shrine of St. Joseph (St. Joseph's Jesuit Catholic Church), 1220 N. 11th Street

7. Which brewing company originally made Falstaff beer?

Lemp

8. In 1922, it was announced that a new high school was being constructed that would bear the name of a famous physician who lived for some years in St. Louis. What was the name of the school?

Beaumont, named for Dr. William Beaumont

9. Who was mayor of St. Louis during the time of the 1904 World's Fair?

Rolla Wells

10. Who succeeded G. Duncan Bauman as publisher of the St. Louis *Globe-Democrat?*

Jeffrey Gluck

11. When the Weatherbird was created, the St. Louis *Post-Dispatch* was in the 500 block of what street?

Olive Street, at 513, the paper's home from 1888 to 1902. The Weatherbird was first printed on February 11, 1901.

12. Which Pope was responsible for making The Old Cathedral a basilica in 1963?

Pope John XXIII. The church opened in 1834.

13. In the early days of St. Louis, who was known as "Le Mère de St. Louis" (the Mother of St. Louis)?

Madame Marie Thérèse Chouteau

14. In what year did the Harold Koplar-designed Zodiac Lounge and Starlight Roof atop the Chase Hotel open? It replaced the Chase Roof Garden, where popular dance bands played under the stars from the '20s?

December, 1940. (Acts performing then included Orrin Tucker and his orchestra, with song stylist Wee Bonnie Baker. They had a hit record at the time, "Oh, Johnny, Oh!")

15. What was the name of the auto agency that immediately preceded the now razed Sewing's Salad Bowl cafeteria at its final location of 3949 Lindell Boulevard? It was a De Soto-Plymouth agency.

St. Louis Motors. The Salad Bowl moved there in 1963 for a very long stay.

16. In the mid-60s, the Frisco Railway ran the only overnight train to and from Tulsa and Oklahoma City. What was the name of the train?

The Meteor

17. Food Center supermarkets were taken over by what chain?

National Food Stores

18. In what mid-County community is Berry's cave?

Brentwood. Access to the cave, in the 8900 block of Manchester Road, has long been sealed. The cave reaches as far as Brentwood Boulevard.

19. In what year was Marx Hardware, at 2501 N. 14th Street, founded?

1875

20. What historic, 1812 home is at Franklinville Farm in Bellefontaine Neighbors? It's located at 10225 Bellefontaine Road.

General Daniel Bissell House

21. What was the massive, man-made structure at what would become the intersection of Broadway and Mound Street?

A ceremonial Indian mound. It became known as the "Big Mound;" and in the mid-19th century it was topped by an attraction called Vauxhall Gardens.

22. What historian and artist compiled and wrote the nationally successful hardback book, *Life on the River?* It was called "a pictorial history of the Mississippi, Missouri and the western river system."

Norbury Wayman

23. The first African-American Missourian to be elected to the United States House of Representatives was a St. Louisan. Who is he?

William Clay

24. The northern terminus for the Bellefontaine streetcar was at the intersection of Robin and W. Florissant Avenues. What street was the end of the line on the south?

Primm Avenue

25. What is today the better-known name for La Petite Riviere of St. Louis?

Mill Creek

26. What firm was the official main sponsor of the St. Louis Bicentennial celebration titled "Under Three Flags?" It ran from September 14th-25th, 1964?

Famous-Barr

27. Jimmy Massucci, one of the designers of, and club owners in, Gaslight Square abandoned the Square to help spearhead a new entertainment area to be known as Laclede's Landing. What was the name of his place on the Landing?

Café Louie. It was at 3rd and Delmar Streets and sported an 1890's French décor.

28. How did the City of Alton get that name?

It was named for the son of Colonel Rufus Easton of St. Louis, who created the street plan for Alton in 1817. The community had started with one log cabin in 1800.

29. What development firm was the first to plan for redevelopment of the St. Louis City Hospital at Lafayette Avenue? The developer dropped the plan, and the property was taken over by the LRA (Land Reutilization Authority).

Pantheon Corporation. The building, constructed in 1905, is now a condominium called "The Georgian." The first hospital at that site opened in 1846.

RABBITT'S TRIVIA GAME

1904: The Fair Year

★ ROUND EIGHTEEN ★

1. What was the name of the railroad that ran within the confines of the 1904 World's Fair grounds?

The intramural railroad

2. At the time of the '04 Fair, what was the name of the street that formed the western boundary of the Fair?

Pennsylvania Avenue. It's now Big Bend Boulevard.

3. What monument was across the walkway at the northern end of the Grand Basin?

The Louisiana Purchase Monument

4. By what method did U. S. president Teddy Roosevelt indicate that the Fair was officially open?

By telegraph. The president sent the signal by activating a gold telegraphic key that was on a dais atop a blue and gold cloth-covered mahogany table at the south end of the East Room of the White House.

5. For how many days did the Fair operate?

215, though some say 216

6. In what year was the Fair's Ferris Observation Wheel dismantled in Chicago for the final time?

1903

7. What State building at the Fair was destroyed by fire on November 19th, 1904?

Missouri

8. Measured by mileage, how long was The Pike?

One mile

9. In what exhibit on The Pike would you have found a large circular slide?

The Temple of Mirth (also called The Foolish House, as well as The Fun Factory)

10. The exterior of the main section of the Palace of Arts, now the St. Louis Art Museum, was constructed of what principal materials?

Bedford limestone and Roman brick

11. In what year did the City of St. Louis buy the Smithsonian Institution's flight cage in Forest Park? It was that organization's gift to The Fair.

1916. The city bought the cage as part of the founding of the new St. Louis Zoo in that year.

12. What building currently stands on the site of the main entrance to the Fair?

The Jefferson Memorial (Missouri Historical Society)

13. The Fair's director of press relations would go on to found the University of Missouri School of Journalism. What was his name?

Walter Williams

14. The bulk of the exteriors of the buildings at the Fair were made of an impermanent substance known as "staff." At what international exposition was staff first used?

The Paris Exposition of 1878

15. Who was the beer baron who committed suicide by gunshot at 9:30 a.m. February 13th, 1904? He served as a board member of the Louisiana Purchase Exposition.

William J. Lemp, at age 68

16. What's the name of the last of the William Pitzman-designed private places? It opened in 1904 and was built at the northwest edge of the Fairgrounds.

Parkview Place

17. What was the name of the official periodic publication of the Fair?

"World's Fair Bulletin"

18. How many states and territories of the United States had buildings, called pavilions, at the Fair?

45

19. The U. S. Secretary of War attended the Fair's inaugural ceremonies here in St. Louis. What was his name?

William Howard Taft

20. Subsequent to the Fair and until 1907, what institution operated the Art Museum of fairgrounds fame?

Washington University

21. Why did the Fair get the nickname "The Ivory City?"

Because the great majority of the buildings were white

22. Name the noted architectural firm that designed the George Washington Hotel at 600 N. Kingshighsway Boulevard. It was built in 1903 specifically for visitors to the Fair.

Eames & Young

23. At the time of the Fair, the Philippines was a territory of what country?

The U.S.A.

24. What brand of beer was called the "World's Fair Beer?"

Lemp. The Lemp Brewing Company pavilion was located beneath the Observation Wheel.

25. Ragtime pianist and composer Scott Joplin wrote "The Cascades" to commemorate the trio of cascades that flowed from the center of Festival Hall down what is now Art Hill. At this time what was Joplin's address?

2658 Morgan (Delmar) Boulevard

26. In what year did Random House originally publish the book *Meet Me in St. Louis?*

1941

27. The gate to what Shaw neighborhood street was erected during the same year as the Fair?

Flora Boulevard (now Flora Place). The six-block street, designed by Julius Pitzman, was based on Henry Shaw's plan that Flora would be a long, landscaped entry to what was then the main entry to Shaw's Garden at Tower Grove Avenue.

28. At the time of the Fair, what animal was depicted on the front of the then-current United States $10 bill?

A bison

29. What is the architectural design term for the 1901 Brookings Hall at Washington University? It was used as the administration building for the Fair.

Gothic

30. Was the Fair's president, David R. Francis, clean-shaven or did he sport a beard or moustache (or both)?

He had a modified handlebar moustache.

MEMORIES

The Beatles Story

★ CHAPTER FOUR ★

THE FIRST BEATLE TO VISIT ST. LOUIS WAS GEORGE HARRISON. Even though we'd given his persistent sister Louise, who lived less than a hundred miles away, no real hope that we'd ever be playing The Beatles, she told us he'd be coming over and she'd like us to meet him. Since he visited her for nearly three weeks, she arranged for him to visit a number of Missouri and Illinois stations, big and small. On the day that he came to call at KXOK, he also had dropped in on WIL at their studios in the Coronado Hotel. He left some records there but really didn't get to talk with anyone other than John Box, the managing director of the station, and his secretary, Harriet Baker, whom he happened to meet at the receptionist's desk, as they were off to lunch. Their programming department said they didn't have time for him.

But, as a favor to Louise, whom we had gotten to know pretty well, I met George and a companion at our Radio Park studios at 1600 N. Kingshighway and escorted them down to an underground tunnel that was part of the complex. You'd get there by moving a stairway from the side of a bandstand in an unused part of our building that we called "the old house." You'd go down several steps to an arched, brick, cavern-like area, which led out under Kingshighway toward Sherman Park. Even though Radio Park is gone, I imagine the strange tunnel still exists. This is where we often, for a lark, took record company people and their artists.

We listened to his records on a small, portable, Mercury phonograph, which we kept on a wooden box next to a candle. Afterward, we drove up to the Bonfire Restaurant at the Carousel Motel just north of Natural Bridge on Kingshighway. We ate "broasted" chicken, served by the restaurant's manager, Ray Gourley. George didn't leave with much hope other than that we promised to play another of their songs on Make It Or Break It.

Interesting to note, there were no screaming fans, and no great entourage, and we didn't even think about taking pictures or to have George record some promotional announcements for us.

RABBITT'S TRIVIA GAME

The Search Is On!

★ ROUND NINETEEN ★

1. Finish this seven-word phrase, etched in stone above the entrance to the St. Louis Art Museum. "Dedicated to art and _____ __ ____."

...free to all."

2. There are two sculpted, marble animals guarding the entrance to Bannister House, the St. Louis U faculty club at 3824 Lindell Boulevard. What are they?

Lions

3. There's a clock tower in midtown, east of Compton Avenue between Olive Street and Laclede Avenue. Name the building on which it's located.

Emerson Performance Center of Harris Stowe University

4. What was the name of the cocktail lounge that was in Laclede Town?

Coach and Four Pub

5. What type of reptiles are depicted in metal on the front of the old J. Arthur Anderson Laundry Building at 4940 Washington Boulevard?

Turtles. There are four of the creatures.

6. What was the name of the nightclub owned by Jordan Chambers, who was dubbed the "Negro Mayor of St. Louis?" The club featured famous African-American performers and was located at 4460 Delmar Boulevard. It was destroyed by fire 1971.

Club Rivera – also known as The Riviera, and earlier as the Showboat

7. What CWE/Midtown area received a marker designating it as an American Historical Landmark?

Gaslight Square

8. What library branch was replaced with the opening of the Schlafly branch at 225 N. Euclid Avenue?

Jacob M. Lashly branch, at 4537 West Pine Boulevard

9. In what decade did the Express Highway open? That's the stretch of today's I-64/40 that ran from Skinker Boulevard to Chouteau Avenue. Was it in the 1920s, 1930s, 1940s or 1950s?

1930s (1937)

10. At 3124 Olive Street, there's a building with a Moorish-design façade that is now a loft apartment building. What was the name of the last commercial occupant at that location?

Morgan Linen Service. Prior to that it was Dinks-Parrish Laundry.

11. What statue "greeted" visitors to the 1904 World's Fair main entrance at Lindell Boulevard and DeBaliviere Avenue?

The statue of King Louis IX. It was later recast in bronze and placed across from the front entrance to the St. Louis Art Museum.

12. What was the name of the Catholic Church at 2913 Locust Street, the site of which is now a vacant lot? They had daily lunches for the public, and handouts were given to the needy at the rectory's back door at 10:00 a.m. every day.

St. Charles Borromeo

13. On what street will you find Municipal Bath House Number 6? This was the final public bath house to be built and the last to close. It operated from 1937 to 1965.

1120 St. Louis Avenue (Near Crown Candy, where you might want to try the Johnny Rabbitt Special Fresh Banana Malt with whipped cream, nuts and nutmeg.)

14. In what year did the St. Louis Fire Department move their headquarters to 1421 N. Jefferson?

1989 (February 15th)

15. Since just before WWI, the Theodore Link-designed Grace United Methodist Church has been at Waterman and Skinker Boulevards, but the church, which was built in 1892, had been constructed at another location. Beginning in 1912, it was dismantled, then rebuilt as it was on its new site. Where was it originally located?

Lindell Boulevard and Newstead Avenue

16. What's the name of the company that resurrected and restored the Coronado Hotel, now apartments, at 3701 Lindell Boulevard?

Restoration St. Louis

17. What now-deceased, notable radio station executive had the license plate of NBC1?

Chuck Norman. The letters stood for "Norman Broadcasting Company."

18. In what building was the public Art Museum located prior to moving to its present location in 1906?

The Washington University School of Fine Arts, at Locust and 19th Streets

19. Before Miss Hullings and long before Dooley's Ltd., what was the name of the grill room and bake shop that occupied the 1st floor and basement restaurant space of the Chemical building at 8th and Olive Streets?

Benish

20. What was the candy company at 612 N. 1st Street? Yellow Jacket candy was one of their brands.

Switzer's Licorice

21. Who is the artist that created the 100-ton "Animals Always" sculpture for the Saint Louis Zoo?

Albert Paley

22. In what year was the Old Courthouse last officially used for regular court proceedings?

1930 (June 21st). The new Civil Courthouse was dedicated the same day, following a parade west on Chestnut Street.

23. For whom is the St. Louis University research building at Grand Boulevard and Chouteau Avenue named?

Edward A. Doisy

24. In what community will you find the St. Louis Regional Airport?

Bethalto, IL

25. On what building will you find a replica of the Daniel Chester French sculpture titled "Peace and Vigilance?"

The Old U.S. Customs House and Post Office downtown. This structure covers the entire city block bounded by Olive, Locust, 8th and 9th Streets. Oh, and the original sculpture is on display in the safety of the interior of the same building.

26. Murphy Lake is located near what major St. Louis street?

Lindell Boulevard. Murphy Lake's in Forest Park between Union Boulevard and Lake Avenue.

27. What local railroad was officially started in 1963?

The Zoo Line Railroad (8/29/63)

28. What was the name of the businessman who founded University City?

Edward Garner Lewis

29. In what hotel was the Terrace Prime Rib Room located?

The Statler, at 9th Street and Washington Avenue. It was a Hilton Hotel at the time.

30. What type business originally occupied the building that houses Frank and Helen's Pizzeria at 8111 Olive St. Rd.?

A drive-thru car wash

31. A large globe of the world can be found at the entrance to what County high school?

Clayton High School

32. How many passengers could the *Admiral* hold when it cruised the Mississippi?

4,400

RABBITT TRIVIA GAME

The Show Must Go On

★ ROUND TWENTY ★

1. In what nightclub did the Compass Players perform?

Crystal Palace

2. For several years, The City Players under Irma Schira Tucker, and then her son, Girard Tucker, held their productions in a closed hotel. Which hotel?

Coronado

3. At what theatre did *St. Louis Blues*, the story of W. C. Handy, have its world premier? The movie starred Nat "King" Cole.

Fox

4. What was the theatre at 517 Chestnut Street that offered a daily fare of both live burlesque and "racy" flicks?

Garrick

5. The West End theatre and Lyric Skydome, later named West End Lyric, was located on what street? The building is no longer standing.

Delmar Boulevard (4119)

6. On Friday, June 17th, 1927, St. Louis' major midtown and downtown theatres advertised special Saturday post-parade programs in honor of what famous person's homecoming?

Charles A. Lindbergh

7. What midtown theatre was once home of Koplar Television productions, Faith Tabernacle and later the Theatre Project Company?

The Sun (its current name)

8. Name the former movie star who, while staying at the Mayfair Hotel, refused to visit the Ambassador theatre to have a photo taken with a group attempting to save the Ambassador....unless she was paid $5,000.

Ginger Rogers

9. Name the man who for years ran the American Theatre and then the Goldenrod Showboat.

Frank Pierson

10. Who is president and general manager of The Muny?

Dennis Reagan

11. Into the 1960s, there were two movie theatres downtown on 6th Street: The Lyric at 116 N. 6th and another at 210 N. 6th. What was the name of the second theatre?

Rivoli (later Towne)

12. St. Ann was home to two major drive-in movie theatres: The Airway was on the north side of St. Charles Rock Rd. and the other was nearby on the south side of the Rock Rd. What was that theatre's name?

St. Ann 4 Screen

13. Who starred in The Muny's 1998 production of *Peter Pan*?

Cathy Rigby

14. Name the local theatre troupe that, among other productions, has staged their "live" spin on movies such as *Plan 9 from Outer Space, Glen or Glenda* and *Planet of the Apes?*

Magic Smoking Monkey Theatre

15. In what metro community will you find the Skyview drive-in theatre?

Belleville

16. Name the person who came from Russia to see the St. Louis World's Fair and while here created a stage make-up called "flexible grease paint?"

Max Factor. His son, Max, Jr., was born here, and the family moved to Los Angeles in 1908.

17. How many stories tall is the office building and retail section of the Tivoli theatre?

Four

18. Wehrenberg Theatres has been in operation longer than any other theatre circuit. What was the first name of the founder of that company?

Fred

19. What theatre, in a former church, hosts an annual cabaret series and is home to the Black Rep?

Grandel

20. What was the principal downtown public building used in the Sci-Fi Channel production "Black Hole?"

St. Louis Soldiers Memorial Military Museum

21. In what theatre did Elvis Presley make his first St. Louis appearance?

Missouri

22. What venue was noted for presenting "old time melodrama?"

Capt. J. W. Menke's Goldenrod Showboat

23. The owner of the hamburger stand at 18th & Olive Streets that was used in the movie *White Palace* wanted to keep that name, but the movie producers said no, so it became the "White Knight." But what was the original name of the place?

Super Sandwich Shop

24. Who wrote the 250-page hardback book titled *100 Years of Reel Entertainment – How Wehrenberg Theatres Became the Longest Running Picture Show in America?*

Steve DeBellis

25. The building housing the Barnard Rubber Stamp Company at 3143 Olive St. was originally a distribution facility and theatre (the Art Theatre) for what major motion picture company? The film company's name is still on the façade behind the Barnard sign.

R.K.O.

RABBITT TRIVIA GAME

The 20's Roar

★ ROUND TWENTY-ONE ★

1. What current radio station traces its history to 1922? It was once WEB.

   WIL-AM 1430

2. In the 1920 census, which city passed St. Louis for the honor of being the 4th largest in the USA?

   Detroit

3. There were 3 major theatres on the east side of Grand Boulevard between Morgan (Delmar) and Washington Avenue. They were the Missouri, the St. Louis (Powell Hall)...but what was the third?

   The New Grand Central. It was on the NE corner of Grand and Lucas Street (now Samuel Shepard Drive). It operated from 1913 to 1933 and was razed in 1957.

4. What was the original (1924) name of the bar and buffet at 8 S. Sarah Street? It became the Scottish Arms in 2005.

   Pacini's Cafe

5. A bond issue for more than $87 million was approved by City voters in 1923 with 20 of 21 propositions passing. The one that failed was for a new attraction in Forest Park. What was it for?

   An aquarium

6. What was the name of the bank located on Hemp Avenue between Manchester Road and Vandeventer Avenue? The office building with the same name is still there.

   Chouteau Trust

7. What downtown movie palace opened in 1924?

Loew's State

8. Name the major oil company that once had its own high rise headquarters downtown?

Shell Oil Company (13th and Locust Streets)

9. Starting in 1923, what transportation company operated double-decker buses in St. Louis?

People's Motorbus Company

10. The Chase, Coronado, Forest Park and Melbourne hotels were among many 1920s buildings designed by what noted St. Louis architect?

Preston J. Bradshaw

11. What was the name of the frozen custard stand at 4224 S. Grand Boulevard prior to its being a Ted Drewes location?

North Pole Frozen Custard, owned by Roy and Cecil Turner

12. In 1929, the City Plan Commission considered creating an airport on two Mississippi River islands. One was Mosenthein; what was the other?

Cabaret Island

13. The *J.S. Deluxe* and the *Saint Paul* were St. Louis-based excursion boats plying the river from the end of WWI into the 1930s. What company owned and operated these boats?

Streckfus Steamers

14. Who was the prominent St. Louisan who in the 1920s was the driving force for the creation of an airfield in Bridgeton?

Albert Bond Lambert

15. What was the name of the hotel, built in 1921, on the SW corner of 18th and Losust Streets? It survived into the 1970s.

Claridge Hotel

MEMORIES

The Beatles Story

★ CHAPTER FIVE ★

ONE OTHER PLACE THAT GEORGE HARRISON, HIS ASSOCIATE, AND I hit when he was in town in '63 was the private entertainment Mecca of local character Johnny Noel. This more or less secret place was around the corner from Radio Park on what was then known as Easton Avenue. It was above Johnny Noel's tire store. The place had a large nightclub with a stage and every kind of instrument, a cocktail lounge, swimming pool, gambling rooms and a professional basketball court, plus a go-kart track on the roof. A few players from the St. Louis Hawks and Baltimore Bullets basketball teams were there at the time. Meeting the longhaired, unknown rocker from England didn't impress them or Johnny Noel. After a walk back to KXOK, Harrison would depart for his sister and her husband Dr. Gordon Caldwell's place in Benton, Illinois, and I wouldn't see him again until I had the great honor of greeting them at the San Francisco airport, staying with them at the San Francisco Hilton, and being the person to introduce the Beatles almost a year later at the Cow Palace in San Francisco.

Oh, I'd mentioned we'd given the Beatles another shot on "Make It Or Break It." It was "She Loves You," and about 90% of the calls said to Break It. We remained convinced they'd never be a hit in the United States. Never say never is good advice.

The next time I'd talk with them would be when they played Busch Stadium in '66.

RABBITT TRIVIA GAME

St. Louis Trivia 101

★ ROUND TWENTY-TWO ★

1. What beer was advertised as "The Choicest Product of the Brewer's Art?" In the late 1960s it was the best-selling brand in St. Louis area.

Falstaff

2. Who was the famous, St. Louis-born star of the silver screen who played the role of "Fagin" in a production of *Oliver* at The Muny?

Vincent Price

3. During what month of 1896 did a major tornado/cyclone rip through much of St. Louis?

May

4. What was the name of the ladies, ready-to-wear store at the NE corner of 7th and Locust streets?

Three Sisters

5. The Arena, the Fox and the Continental building all opened in what year?

1929

6. Ry-Krisp was originally the product of what major area company?

Ralston-Purina

7. What downtown building is considered to be without a "back door", as it covers a full city block with entrances on all 4 streets?

Railway Exchange Building

8. On what street was the Holiday drive-in theatre located?

Page Boulevard (9900)

9. Name the St. Louis-born poet who wrote "Wynken, Blynken and Nod."

Eugene Field

10. Lloyds of London insured St. Louis stripper Evelyn West's "Treasure Chest" for how much?

$50,000

11. What band had the original hit of "The St. Louis Blues March?"

Glenn Miller Orchestra

12. What long-time "made in St. Louis" product used the slogan "N-R Tonight, Tomorrow Alright?" N-R signs still grace the company's HQ building downtown.

Nature's Remedy, sister product of Tums

13. What slogan was used to promote Tums?

"Tums for the Tummy"

14. What is the corporate name of St. Louis' second-biggest brewer?

St. Louis Brewery – brewer of the Schlafly brand

15. At what intersection was the entrance to the commercial Cherokee Cave located?

Cherokee Street and Broadway. It was directly east of the Chatillon-De Menil mansion.

16. What was the name of the last bank to operate from the tallest office building in South St. Louis?

Allegiant Bank. The building, at Grand Boulevard and Gravois Road, was constructed for South Side National Bank.

17. The Beaux Arts and Metropolitan buildings are located on what street?

N. Grand Boulevard

18. What drive-in restaurant chain billed their carhops as "The Boys in the Orange Jackets?"

The Parkmoor

19. There are 2 public caves in Leasburg, MO. One is Onondaga, but what's the name of the other?

Cathedral Cave

20. Name the late barber/hair stylist who is the only person in the world to be in both the Barbering Hall of Fame and the Cosmetology Hall of Fame. His shop is still in operation.

Earl Roach (Earl's in Clayton)

21. What was the name of the "made in St. Louis" movie that had its world premier at the Tivoli theatre in July 2005?

"Hooch & Daddio"

22. There's a large, framed photo-portrait of the late Robert Hyland, for many years head of KMOX Radio, in the lobby of what medical institution?

The Hyland Center at St. Anthony's Hospital

23. What was the name of the town that was abandoned because of Dioxin contamination?

Times Beach

24. What was the name of the hamburger stand-type restaurant on Lemay Ferry Road that issued death certificates with your food?

Art Wild's Palace of Poison

25. Immediately before leaving television for academia, Al Wiman was a reporter for what station?

KSDK (He had previously been with KMOV)

26. At what institution will you find the contents of the former Museum of Quackery? This museum had been housed in the St. Louis Medical Society building.

St. Louis Science Center

27. What was the original name of the hospital that is now Barnes-Jewish Hospital West on Olive Boulevard?

Faith Hospital

28. In what decade of the 20th century did the Soldiers Memorial Military Museum open?

1930s

29. What was the original name of the older section of downtown's Renaissance Hotel?

Statler Hotel – later the Statler-Hilton and then the Gateway Hotel

30. Name the second-oldest bridge across the Mississippi River at St. Louis. It opened on April 19th, 1890 and is still in use.

Merchants Bridge. This is a railroad-only structure.

RABBITT TRIVIA GAME

We Mean Business!

★ ROUND TWENTY-THREE ★

1. What was the name of the major, national, upscale retailer that operated from a three-story building in the CWE?

   Saks Fifth Avenue

2. What major jewelry store occupied part of the first floor of the now-demolished Century Building?

   Mermod-Jaccard-King

3. At what CWE intersection was General Van and Storage located? It's an office building today.

   The SW corner of Euclid Avenue and Delmar Boulevard

4. What was the name of the two-story, red brick building on the NE corner of Grand and Lindell Boulevards?

   The Marina Building

5. What's the official name of COCA?

   The Center of Creative Art

6. The Circus Snack Bar was at one time in what CWE hotel that has been brought back to life as an apartment building?

   Forest Park Hotel

7. What's the new name of the old Northland Shopping Center in Jennings?

   Buzz Westfall Plaza

8. What was the principal food item canned at Sansone's restaurant, 3724 Union Boulevard across from the Fisher Body plant?

   Sansone's Sea Seasoned Turtle Chili

9. From 1947 to 1973, the late Julian Miller published a local, monthly magazine from his headquarters in the Chase hotel. What was the name of the magazine?

Prom *magazine*

10. The Goody Train restaurant, Dorr & Zeller ice cream and caterers, Little Las Vegas, Toddle House, Sorrento's and radio station KCFM were all at various times on what West End street?

DeBaliviere Avenue

11. Who is the St. Louisan who owns the Oaklawn Racetrack in Hot Springs, Arkansas? This is the oldest family-operated racetrack in America.

Charles Cella

12. What railroad operated a train called the "Green Diamond" out of Union Station?

Illinois Central

13. What men's retail clothing store on S. Broadway has been in the same location for more than 80 years?

Kleb's (It was previously called Louis J. Kleb's.)

14. What William B. Ittner-designed St. Louis city public school was saved from becoming a parking lot for a Walgreen's store?

Theresa School at 1517 S. Theresa Avenue. Amy and Amrit Gill have successfully converted it into a 35-unit loft apartment building.

15. Name the "Born in St. Louis" celebrity who owns a production company called "A Bird and a Bear Entertainment."

Cedric (Cedric The Entertainer) Kyles

16. New York's Omnicom Group, specialists in advertising, marketing and public relations, now own 2 born and bred in St. Louis firms. One is the Rodgers Townsends ad agency...what's the other?

Fleishman Hillard PR.

17. What real estate mogul once published an underground newspaper named *Xanadu*?

Pete Rothschild

18. What is the architectural name for the female figures gracing either side of the downtown Famous-Barr (Macy's) entrances?

Caryatids

19. Who anchors the FSN Network's "The Midwest Sports Report," which moved production from Pittsburgh to St. Louis in 2006?

Pat Harris

20. What radio personality wrote the book *City of Gabriels: The History of Jazz in St. Louis, 1895-1973?*

Dennis Owsley, who has conducted the show "Jazz Unlimited" on KWMU since 1983.

21. The Black Cat theatre at 2810 Sutton Ave. in Maplewood is in 2 buildings that for years housed a supermarket. What was the name of the grocery chain that used these structures?

Bettendorf

22. What's the name of the Chase Park Plaza memorabilia room located in the lower level of the Chase? The room's available for viewing through the concierge.

The Legacy Room. (I'm proud to say I designed the room and collected the materials displayed therein.)

23. What bank annually shows a movie in their lobby that's related to that bank's history?

Southwest Bank at Kingshighway Blvd. and Southwest Ave. The film is the 1959 "The Great St. Louis Bank Robbery," which dramatized a stick-up at that location.

24. What firm funded the plaques honoring some of our city's automobile history that have been placed on a number of buildings in the original Automobile Row on Locust St. in Midtown?

Hilliker Corporation

25. In what Illinois community will you find a place known as the "R-Pizza Farm?"

Dow. It's an 8 miles from Alton. The crops of the farm, which are all familiar pizza toppings, are grown within a 150-foot circle divided by 8 "slices". They even bake and serve pizza for visitors.

RABBITT TRIVIA GAME

Triviarama

★ ROUND TWENTY-FOUR ★

1. In 1963, Matilda Laumeier initiated talks regarding the donation of her land to be used for a County park. At that time, who was the director of St. Louis County Parks?

Wayne C. Kennedy

2. Who was the local person who produced the musical revue "Americans in Paris," which was presented at the Chase Club of the Chase Hotel in the 1950s?

Harold Koplar

3. Name the sports announcer who in 2006 paraphrased philosopher George Santayana by saying: "Like the guy said, if you wanna know what's gonna happen tomorrow, pay attention to what happened today."

Mike Shannon

4. The late, internationally acclaimed jazz trumpeter Maynard Ferguson credited what St. Louis dentist for helping him to continue his career after it almost ended because of severe dental problems?

Dr. Mark Meyers. Even though Ferguson lived in California, he traveled to St. Louis for dental work for the last eight years of his life.

5. From the teens into the '50s, our city was home to three original Garavelli's locations. One was at DeBaliviere and DeGiverville Avenues, another was at 3606 Olive Street, across from the Continental Building. Where was the third? In the mid 1950s, it was the first Garavelli's to close.

3559 Olive Street, just east of the Metropolitan Building

6. Who hosted "The Breakfast Serial" program, which ran on St. Louis radio for many years? It first aired in the early '70s on KSLQ, then in the late '90s on WRTH.

Jonnie King

7. Name the CBS-TV anchor who hails from Rock Hill.

Russ Mitchell

8. How did explorer Meriwether Lewis die?

Most reports say he committed suicide by using a gun and knife

9. The Roberts Lofts on the Plaza building was previously home to the headquarters of what St. Louis institution?

St. Louis Public Schools

10. Who was manager of Kiel Auditorium and Opera House between 1978 and 1981? He then became director of the Cervantes Convention Center until 1984. Here's a hint: he co-owned a family-named bar and grill that opened in 1916 and remains in business today.

Joe Failoni

11. Cornell Haynes, Jr., is better known by what name?

Nelly

12. How many members of the troubled Lemp family took their lives in the house now known as the Lemp Mansion?

Three. As the story goes, they still spend some time there.

13. Who was the first person to be miraculously healed at St. Joseph's Jesuit Catholic Church at 1220 N. 11th St.? (It's now the Shrine of St. Joseph.)

Ignatius Strecker, a German immigrant who recovered from a terminal illness after he venerated a relic of Peter Claver. Peter Claver would be canonized following this miracle.

14. In 1699, what area village was established by priests from the Holy Family Missions in Quebec? This date makes it the oldest permanent European settlement in the Mississippi Valley.

Cahokia

15. What was the name of the Chevrolet dealership at 4035 Lindell Boulevard in the '50s and '60s? The firm is still around.

Weber Chevrolet

16. Dad's Original Scotch Oatmeal cookies were sold for the first time in what year?

1938

17. What was the name of the movie theatre at 1860 S. 13th St.? It would become the Maryland Pentecostal Church.

Maryland

18. The movie *Hail! Hail! Rock 'n Roll,* filmed principally at the Fox Theatre, was in part created to celebrate what birthday of the film's star, Chuck Berry?

60th

19. What's the name of the private South County museum owned by Greg Rhomberg of Nu-Way Concrete Forms? The museum collection is dedicated to items from the start of the Industrial Revolution through the 1970s, with an emphasis on St. Louis-related artifacts.

The Antique Warehouse

20. Ronnie's Ice Cream and Quezel Sorbets are manufactured in what South City apartment-hotel building?

The Saum, at 1919 S. Grand Blvd.

21. Of what material is the statue of Mary Our Lady of the River at Portage des Sioux made?

Fiberglass

22. Where in St. Louis during the 1940s were the bones of the extinct peccary, *platygonus compressus,* discovered?

In the Lemp (or Cherokee) caverns

23. Why was the section of I-55 near Meramec Bottom Rd. named "The Thomas G. Smith, Jr. Memorial Highway?"

Smith was a St. Louis County police officer who was struck and killed by an automobile in that area in 1997.

24. The Chouteau Society recognizes donors of planned gifts for what St. Louis institution?

Missouri Historical Society

25. Who took command of Jefferson Barracks in 1855?

Robert E. Lee

26. When the groundbreaking ceremony took place in 1953 for Cardinal Glennon Children's Hospital, what was the name of the drug store in the office building catercorner to the hospital?

Grand-Park Pharmacy

27. When the 2nd Busch Stadium was built, what street was the eastern terminus for Highway 40?

18th Street

28. What was the name of the fire alarm system used by the City of St. Louis Fire Department from 1858 until 1977?

The Gamewell Fire Alarm System

29. What's the name of the St. Louis-area parent company of the Broyhill brand of furniture?

Furniture Brands International, based in Clayton

30. What Forest Park dining spot offers water and dog biscuits for canine "customers?"

The Boathouse

31. What was the name of the cruise ship that was used to evacuate St. Louis University's president, The Rev. Lawrence Biondi, S.J., and more than a thousand other Americans from Lebanon to Cyprus in the 2006 Middle East War?

Orient Queen

32. Name the famed St. Louis barrister who spoke on behalf of the Bar Association at the closing of the courts at the Old Courthouse in 1930. At the time, he proposed the creation of a museum to preserve the collection of the court's documents. He had been admitted to the bar in 1877.

Isaac H. Lionberger

33. The St. Louis Hispanic Festival was originally located in what area park?

Faust

34. Who hit a home run for the Cards against the Cubs in game one of the 1951 season at Sportsman's Park?

Joe Garagiola

35. There are seven hotels along 4th Street in downtown St. Louis. They are: Millenium, Drury Plaza, Adam's Mark, Radisson, Hilton Downtown and WS. Name the seventh.

Hampton Inn (originally Bel Air East)

36. What McDonnell-Douglas passenger airliner had its first flight in 1970?

DC-10

37. What St. Louis movie theatre's name started with the letter "Y?"

The Yale, at 3700 Minnesota

38. What's the St. Louis phonetic pronunciation of Bellefontaine?

bell FOUN ten

39. Who were the brothers that operated the Ambassador theatre, and others, in St. Louis, before they headed to great fame and fortune in Hollywood?

Charlie and Spyros Skouras

40. In its heyday, who handled the PR for Gaslight Square? She's long been big with the CWE Association.

Mary Bartley

41. Who was the baseball player from Breese, IL, who was in the majors for 13 years, hit over .300 five times and played in three World Series? He once led the National League in hitting.

Second baseman Larry Doyle. He played for the New York Giants and the Chicago Cubs. He played from 1907 to 1920.

42. What was the full name of the college that moved from the Dutchtown South neighborhood in 1961?

Maryville College of the Sacred Heart

43. What artist had his monumental (but portable) steel sculptures on display through 2006 by Forest Park's Grand Basin?

Bernar Venet of France

44. What position did Roger Wehrli play for the Football Cardinals from '69-'82?

Cornerback

45. Who owned La Sala, the Mexican "hacienda" that was located at 513 Olive St.?

Steve Apted (of Miss Hullings/Cheshire Inn & Lodge fame)

46. In what year did Webster Groves celebrate its centennial?

1996

47. What's the name of the St. Louis-made product used for cleaning wallpaper? It's pink and has a consistency similar to Silly Putty.

Abosorene. The company is located at 2141 Cass Ave., and for years before that was at 1609 N. 14th St.

48. Who was the 18-year news veteran of KMOX radio who alleged that he was fired for union activities in 1974?

Doug Newman

49. The 19th-century St. Louis Four Courts building and City Jail covered a full city block. It was bounded by Clark, Eleventh, Twelfth and what other street?

Spruce

50. Jazz singer Denise Thimes is the daughter of what legendary radio disc jockey?

Lou "Fatha" Thimes

RABBITT TRIVIA GAME

Lookin' Back. Way Back!

★ ROUND TWENTY-FIVE ★

1. What was the name of the historic tavern and inn on 2nd Street between Myrtle and Spruce Streets that opened in 1816 and remained in operation until 1939, when it fell victim to the land clearance for the Jefferson National Expansion Memorial Park?

Green Tree Tavern

2. In what year did the Marquis de Lafayette visit our fair city?

1825

3. St. Louis' first electric lights were installed in what restaurant?

Tony Faust's

4. What name has been given by scientists to the Indian mound builders who once lived in this area?

The Mississippians

5. What is the full name of the founder of St. Louis?

Pierre Laclede Liguest

6. Name the once-famous movie actor born here in 1879. He appeared in 76 films bewteen 1911 and 1945. He was once president of the Players Club of St. Louis.

King Baggott. He died July 17, 1945.

7. Why did Henry Shaw have a high stone wall built on the east and part of the north side of his garden?

To prevent winds from injuring the then-recently planted garden

8. Who was the first governor of the state of Missouri?

Alexander McNair

9. The first high school west of the Mississippi River exclusively for African-Americans opened here in 1875. What school was it?

Sumner

10. For what monarch was Antoine Soulard employed as a surveyor?

The King of Spain

11. What river island was frequently used for dueling?

Bloody Island. It was on the Illinois side of the river and is now part of E. St. Louis.

12. What was the exact date of the disastrous New Madrid earthquake?

December 17, 1811. It caused only minor damage in St. Louis.

13. Who donated the 2 blocks that became a public market in the Soulard neighborhood?

Antoine Soulard's widow, Julia

14. What firm originally occupied the 1873 Raeder Place building in Laclede's Landing?

The Christian Peper tobacco company

15. In what year was St. Louis University's school of medicine chartered?

1836

16. The Daniel Boone home in Defiance, built by Daniel and his son Nathan, is in what architectural style?

Georgian

17. Who was the soon-to-be-famous person who stayed at Scott's Hotel on October 28, 1847? The inn was at the SW corner of 3rd and Market Streets.

Abraham Lincoln

18. The original 1841 Planters House hotel was so named as materials accidentally arrived with the name "Planters House" imprinted on them. What was to have been the name of the hotel?

Lucas House

19. What was the name of the first bank in St. Louis? It was incorporated in 1813.

Bank of St. Louis

20. What was the original name of the institution located at 9th and Washington that would become St. Louis University?

St. Louis College

21. What was the full name of the newspaper editor, religious leader and abolitionist who was murdered in Alton in 1837?

Elijah Parish Lovejoy

22. What was the name of St. Louis' first daily newspaper? It started publication in 1834.

The Herald

23. Immediately prior to the establishment of Benton Park, for what purpose was that property used?

A cemetery

24. The *Zebulon M. Pike* was the first steamboat to dock in St. Louis. This occured during what year?

1817

25. What area community was nicknamed "Vide Poche?" *Vide Poche* translates to "Empty Pockets."

Carondelet

MEMORIES

The St. Louis Picture Show

FIRST CAME THE FLUTTERING IMAGES PROJECTED IN THE NICKELODEONS; makeshift storefront "theatres" with kitchen or folding chairs, an upright "piana," and a "magic lantern" flashing moving images on a painted white square, or a sheet, at the back of a darkened room. At the beginning, when Fred Wehrenberg and others got the film business going here, owners of legitimate stage houses, burlesque and vaudeville venues, operatic, minstrel, lecture and concert halls considered celluloid a curiosity and no competition. But even though the pictures were without sound, color, clarity or a "voice," customers continued to be fascinated with film, and these fledgling flickers quickly caught on.

The simplicity of this new entertainment allowed early exhibitors, mostly mom and pop operators, to fulfill the American dream of the entrepreneur as they raised their screens, often as an ancillary operation to a saloon. It wouldn't be long before musicians, singers, lecturers, vaudevillians and sundry thespians, as well as theatre impresarios, became rightly wary of the increasing interest in the picture shows.

It didn't happen overnight, but within a very few years, the small neighborhood "shows" prospered and moved out of back rooms and into theatres of their own, often retrofitted existing buildings. The showmen, such as Sam Koplar, put up fancy façades, electric signs and marquees and used names such as Cinderella, Ritz, White Way, Peerless and Columbia. Interiors sported lobbies, concessions (supplied at times by a neighboring candy shop), permanent seating, velvet drapes, murals and chandeliers.

Although these mostly neighborhood houses were small by downtown theatre standards, they emanated excitement and presented a window to the world that the stage could not produce. The silver screen images were now often accompanied by a violinist and drummer joining the pianist; and, as new, larger theatres were built, full orchestras were employed to play the score provided by the motion picture companies. By the twenties, great pipe organs, many made by Wurlitzer, were actually built into theatres such as the Empress and Fox. In those days, a dime got you a lot of music and magic to go with your movie. Of course a dime then was worth more than a dime today. For example, 18 cents would get you a roast prime rib of beef at the Forum cafeteria across from Famous-Barr, and the White Line cleaners on Chippewa would dry clean any two garments for a buck.

By the Great War, most exhibitors had expanded to multiple locations, usually in the vicinity of their original operation, as "agreements" were made not to invade another's territory. As the '20s started to roar, the movies were still silent, but every self-respecting neighborhood had at least one movie house. The common practice of utilizing existing edifices for movie houses was passé, and structures specially built for the showing of films became the norm. The large movie palaces, such as the Missouri, St. Louis, Ambassador, Fox and Loew's State were constructed with ample stage and fly space and complete with dressing rooms, as they were designed to mount both stage and screen presentations. As the theatres presented vaudeville acts between movies, Masters of Ceremony became local celebrities; examples were Ed Lowery at the Ambassador and Frank Fay at the Missouri. These and others would have multi-year runs and were as much a draw as the flicks and stage acts. Ed eventually left for Tinsel Town, where he fizzled, but became a successful Beverly Hills upscale hotelier. Fay married Barbara Stanwyck here in '27, at the city clerk's house on Magnolia Avenue and S. Kingshighway Boulevard (the house with the red steps). They "honeymooned" at the Coronado Hotel. Frank Fay, by the way, starred as "Elwood P. Dowd" in *Harvey* on Broadway but was snubbed by Hollywood. The film role went to Jimmy Stewart.

Early theatre air cooling was created by electric fans, which proved pretty ineffective in the sultry summer months, so, many movie-house owners obtained property adjoining their movie houses for an "airdome." The airdome was an outdoor, walk-in theatre for use during those pre-air conditioning summer nights. The Princess and its adjoining lot can still be seen in the 2800 block of Pestalozzi Street, as can The Fairy on Dr. M. L. King Drive at Blackstone Avenue. There were some airdomes with no adjoining theatre building, such as the Armo, on Morganford Road just a bit south of Arsenal Street. One of the side "benefits" of the airdome occurred as the film unreeled under the stars; an usher would use a hand sprayer to fog the space, and the customer, with a DDT sprayer, warded off mosquitoes. The last major theatre to still employ wall fans to boost its air-conditioning system was the Missouri, at 626 N. Grand Boulevard.

Some theatres, such as the Missouri, Melba, Shubert, Maplewood and Tivoli were built with the auditorium adjoining an office building, while others, such as the Orpheum (American), St. Louis, Macklind, Shaw, O'Fallon, Norside, Studio and Tower were free-standing theatres. The only theatre to have been built completely inside an office building was the Ambassador at 7th and Locust Streets.

Movie-house construction continued at a steady pace until the Great Depression. Then came World War II. So between 1930 and 1947, the only major movie house to be built was the Esquire. Some small houses, such as the Roxy on Wherry Avenue, also were built during that period. One of several theatres planned during that dark time but never constructed was the Hampton Village theatre, which had been designed in the Williamsburg style and intended to be built about where the Schnuck's store is located today. The first drive-in theatre, simply called the Drive-In theatre (later the Manchester), opened just before WWII. It was where West County Center is today.

The first post-WWII movie theatre to be built was the Crest, which was located at 8800 Gravois in Affton and opened in '47. Several other new houses were on the drawing boards but didn't make it to construction, as the movie industry was knocked for a loop by television, which came to our town in 1947 courtesy of KSD and the St. Louis *Post-Dispatch*.

At the mid-point of the 20th century, some 114 theatres were operating in greater St. Louis, and many of these old buildings still stand, filled with ghostly memories of Saturday serials, "dish nights," double bills, cartoons, comedies, newsreels and many first kisses. Some of these places left over from the past include:

★ the Columbia at Columbia and Edwards, now the residence and studio of an artist

★ the Family on Shaw is used as a food firm's warehouse

★ the Grand in Alton is used for storage, and for some years was a Halloween "haunted theatre"

★ the Shaw at 39th and Shaw has been a drug store, food store and medical office

★ the Beverly (later the Fine Arts) is a Chinese restaurant

★ the Macklind, on Arsenal east of Sublette, has housed a plumbing and a heating and air conditioning firm

★ the O'Fallon at Hyde Park is an empty shell, as is the Avalon on S. Kingshighway

★ the Ozark in Webster Groves, the Brentwood in Brentwood and the Osage (Kirkwood) in Kirkwood all house businesses

★ the Virginia on Virginia is a church

★ Clayton's Shady Oak almost became a jazz club, but it's still waiting for re-use

★ the Savoy (Crowne) in Ferguson is a banquet facility

★ the Lemay on Lemay Ferry Road, which had been used for sporting events, is empty

★ the Melvin, on Chippewa near Compton, has had several uses, including that of a classic car storage facility and a church

The Melba on S. Grand, the Missouri on N. Grand and the Cinderella on Cherokee have been razed, though their office building "fronts" are still in place. There are others for you to find, but many are simply gone. These include the Granada, Ritz, Tower, Norside, Lindell, Kingsland, Roxy, Empress, World, Senate, Rivoli (Towne),

Gravois, Trans-Lux (Martin) Cinerama, Maplewood, Congress, Lafayette, Compton, Princess, Bremen, King Bee, Maffit, Aubert, West End Lyric, Apollo, Pageant, Merry Widow, White Way, Richmond, Powhatan, Plymouth, Rio, Uptown (Embassy), Lowell and Strand. And there are dozens more.

ST. LOUIS' OWN

★ *Johnny Rabbitt* ★

THE MAN, THE MYTH, THE LEGEND.

NOT NECESARILY IN THAT ORDER. St. Louis radio legend Johnny Rabbitt, aka Ron Elz, has been a quintessential part of the St. Louis radio scene for more than five decades.

Inducted into the Rock 'N Roll Hall of Fame in Cleveland for his work on St. Louis' own KXOX, KSHE, WRTH and WIL-FM, Rabbitt now works for Legends 1430 WIL AM. As the first GM of KSHE radio, he created the progressive rock format. He was the first person in America to completely program a radio station (KADI) by computer. He has received dozens of honors thoughout his career, including a "Lifetime Achievement Award" from A.I.R. (Achievement in Radio). He founded the Media Archives of the Missouri Historical Society.

He is a consummate historian and trivia buff on all things St. Louis. Rabbitt hosts several St. Louis trivia or history-related events each year, including the annual Missouri Historical Society's Trivia Challenge and The History Museum's "Spirits of St. Louis Ghost Tours." His local trivia questions are aired each day on WIL-AM and on Channel 5's "Show Me St. Louis."

His love of St. Louis is evidenced in the numerous St. Louis restaurants that have "Johnny Rabbitt Specials" on their menus.

He grew up on Flora Place in South St. Louis City and has lived with his wife, Gwen, in St. Louis Hills for more than 35 years.